WHY YOU SHOULD BELIEVE IN THE TRINITY

WHY YOU SHOULD BELIEVE IN THE TRINITY

An Answer to Jehovah's Witnesses

Robert M. Bowman, Jr.

BAKER BOOK HOUSE
Grand Rapids, Michigan 49516

Fourth printing, October 1990

Printed in the United States of America

The New American Standard Bible (NASB) is used as the basis for this study. Other translations used are the New World Translation (NWT), the New International Version (NIV), and the King James Version (KJV).

Library of Congress Cataloging-in-Publication Data

Bowman, Robert M., Jr.
    Why you should believe in the Trinity : an answer to Jehovah's
  Witnesses / Robert M. Bowman, Jr.
      p. cm.
    Includes bibliographical references.
    ISBN 0-8010-0981-2
    1. Jehovah's Witnesses—Controversial literature.   2. Trinity.
  I. Title.
  BX8526.5.B69   1989
  231'.044—dc20   89-39309
                                                CIP

Contents

Introduction
Before You Reject the Trinity

S*hould You Believe in the Trinity?* This is the question posed by the title of a recent publication of the Jehovah's Witnesses (hereafter abbreviated "JWs" for brevity's sake). Their 32-page booklet argues that the Trinity is an apostate doctrine inspired by the devil and resulting from the influence of paganism on Christianity.

If the arguments of the JW booklet are sound, the doctrine of the Trinity should be rejected by all Christians. However, if those arguments are not sound, the possibility ought to be considered that the Trinity is a biblical and Christian doctrine after all.

This book does not offer a thorough or exhaustive study of the doctrine of the Trinity. Instead, it offers brief responses to the claims of the JW booklet and, in so doing, presents a summary of the biblical teaching on the Trinity.

Because this book has as its focus the JWs' denial of the Trinity, it cannot be considered a complete work on the subject. There are various aspects of the doctrine of the Trinity that are not addressed in this book. However, certain sections of the book should be of interest to people who are not concerned with the JWs. For example, the discussion in chapter 3, "The Church and the Trinity," should be of interest to all who are wondering about the origin of trinitarian formulations.

Some JWs may dislike the idea of reading a book, such as this, which criticizes one of their publications. They may feel that they are being "picked on" because this book singles them out and criticizes them and their beliefs. They may reject this book as "anti-Witness" literature and therefore refuse to read it.

That is their privilege. However, it should be noted that the JW booklet to which this book responds is itself completely negative and critical. The whole purpose of that booklet is to criticize belief in the Trinity. The doctrine is said to be completely pagan and those who believe it to be apostate, dishonoring God, and ignoring his true nature. All this book is meant to do is to explain the biblical basis of faith in the Trinity and to answer the specific accusations of the JW booklet. In fact, this book is more positive than the booklet, as it offers some positive reasons for believing in the Trinity (rather than simply negative reasons for *not* believing in the JWs' doctrines about God).

Quotations from the Bible are made without identifying the translation if most translations read virtually the same. Otherwise I have used the abbreviation NWT when citing from the *New World Translation of the Holy Scriptures* (Watchtower Bible and Tract Society, 1984), and NASB when citing from the *New American Standard Bible* (Lockman Foundation, 1977).

Throughout this book reference will be made to scholarly sources misused or misrepresented in the JW booklet. These misrepresentations are pointed out in the interest of giving people all of the facts relevant to evaluating the statements of the scholars in question. Scholars, like every-one else, are fallible, sinful people, with prejudices, precon-ceptions, and misunderstandings. They are often right in what they say, but they are also often wrong; perhaps most often they are only partially right. The reader is urged to weigh everything these scholars have said, everything the JW booklet says, and everything this book says, in the light of Scripture (Acts 17:11; 1 Thess. 5:21).

Comments, questions, and criticisms are welcome, and may be addressed to the author in care of Christian Research Institute, P.O. Box 500, San Juan Capistrano, CA 92693-0500.

1

▲▽▲▽▲▽▲▽▲▽▲▽▲▽▲▽▲▽▲▽▲▽▲▽▲▽▲▽ ▲▽▲

Understanding the Trinity

Getting the Doctrine Straight

Before we can legitimately defend or criticize the doctrine of the Trinity, we ought to do our best to understand it. The place to begin in this endeavor is to define our terms. In this chapter we shall base our definition of the Trinity on the Athanasian Creed.

The simplest way to define the Trinity is to say that it is one God in three persons. Thus the Athanasian Creed speaks of the Trinity as both "one God" and "three Persons." But this definition needs to be expanded if misunderstanding is to be avoided.

Trinitarians (people who believe in the Trinity) hold very firmly and without compromise to belief in one God. The Father, Son, and Holy Spirit are not three Gods. (Mormons, who believe that they *are* three Gods, claim to believe in the Trinity but make it very clear that they reject the traditional doctrine of the Trinity in any form.) The Athanasian Creed makes this point repeatedly: "And yet they are not three Gods, but one God.... So we are forbidden by the catholic [universal] faith to say, there are three Gods or three

Lords." The God worshiped by trinitarians is the one and only God; they recognize no other gods at all. Jesus is not another god alongside God; he is God, together with the Father and the Holy Spirit.

The JWs frequently criticize the Trinity as if it denied the oneness of God. For example, *Should You Believe in the Trinity?* [1] expresses the view of Witnesses, "that the Trinity doctrine is false, that Almighty God stands alone as a separate, eternal, and all-powerful being" (p. 3; hereafter, parenthetical page citations refer to the JW booklet *Should You Believe in the Trinity?*). But trinitarians believe that Almighty God is alone eternal and all-powerful. The biblical teaching "that God alone is the Almighty, the Creator, separate and distinct from anyone else" (p. 12), is thought by JWs to contradict the Trinity, whereas it is in full agreement with it. The antitrinitarian writer L.L. Paine is quoted with approval when he criticizes the Trinity for departing from the "strict monotheism" of the Bible (p. 12)—despite the fact that trinitarianism holds strictly to monotheism (belief in one God). The question is asked, "Does it honor God to call anyone his equal?" (p. 30), as if the Trinity taught that Jesus was an individual apart from God yet equal to him, whereas the Trinity teaches that Jesus *is* God.

Ironically, it is JWs who deny monotheism. They believe that in addition to the "only true God" (John 17:3), and besides the many false gods, there are many creatures who are rightly honored as "gods" under Jehovah God. (We will return to this point in chapter 4.)

Another aspect of God's oneness is the fact that there are no separations or divisions or partitions in God. The trinitarian doctrine holds that God is a single infinite being, transcending the bounds of space and time, having no body either material or spiritual (except the body that the Son assumed in becoming a man). Thus, the trinitarian God has no parts. You cannot divide infinite being into components. The Athanasian Creed affirms that God is not divided by the three persons when it states that the trinitarian faith does not allow for "dividing the substance" (using "substance" to mean the essence or being of God). The three persons, consequently, are not three parts of God, but three personal distinctions within God, each of whom is fully God.

The JWs and other antitrinitarians frequently criticize the Trinity as if it taught or implied that the Father, Son, and Holy Spirit were three parts, components, or divisions in God. Thus, the Holy Spirit is said to be "No Part of a Trinity" (p. 22). The idea that Jesus was "part of a Trinity" is criticized as impossible (p. 23). The word *part* is used repeatedly in the JW booklet to designate persons in the Trinity. The point is made that "if God were composed of three persons" the Bible would have made that clear (p. 13)—whereas the Trinity denies that God is "composed" of any parts at all.

So far we have concentrated on explicating what trinitarians mean when they say that the Trinity is "one God." But the statement that this one God is "three persons" is also one that has often been misunderstood. People often assume that "person" is used to refer to a separate individual being, which would imply that three divine persons were three Gods. The belief in three Gods, called *tritheism*, has always been condemned by trinitarian Christians. We have already noted the Athanasian Creed's clear denial of tritheism. If "person" is used to mean a separate individual being, then in that sense trinitarians frankly would confess to believing that God is one "person."

However, there is another sense of the word *person* that focuses not on separate existence but on relationship; trinitarians believe that the Father, Son, and Holy Spirit are three "persons" in the sense that each is aware of the others, speaks to the others, and loves and honors the others. Thus, God may be described as "one person" or as "three persons," depending on the meaning of "persons." To avoid confusion, however, trinitarians have traditionally agreed to use the word *person* to refer to the Father, Son, and Holy Spirit as distinct from one another. This is the practice followed in the Athanasian Creed.

Trinitarians recognize that God speaks in the Bible as one "person," in the sense of a single personal being when addressing mankind or speaking of his relation to the world. Thus, God refers to himself as "I," and is addressed by humans as "you" in the singular. This is no embarrassment to the trinitarian belief, but fits it perfectly, since trinitarians believe that the three "persons" are one divine being.

Also fitting perfectly with the doctrine of the Trinity is the fact that the Father and the Son speak to and of one another as distinct persons. It is simply a misunderstanding to ask whether trinitarians believe that Jesus prayed to himself when he addressed the Father. This may be an embarrassing question to ask *monarchians* (who deny the Trinity and teach that Jesus is God the Father), but trinitarians simply answer that Jesus the Son prayed to the Father. Trinitarianism recognizes each of the three persons as distinct, not to be confused with one another. Thus, the Athanasian Creed states that trinitarian faith does not allow for "confounding the Persons."

Finally, something needs to be said about the question of the submission of the Son to the Father. No trinitarian questions that when Christ was on earth he lived in submission to God the Father. The Father in heaven was exalted while the Son was humble; the Father was greater than Christ (John 14:28). Christ's human nature was not itself divine; the manhood of Christ was created, and therefore

Christ as man had to honor the Father as his God. Thus, the Athanasian Creed states that Christ is "equal to the Father as touching his Godhead and inferior to the Father as touching his manhood." There is no question from a trinitarian perspective that, as man, Christ was in submission to the Father.

Yet this submission evidently transcends the historical life of Jesus on earth. He was *sent* by the Father into the world (1 John 4:9), implying that in some sense Christ was in submission to the Father before becoming a man. Yet, in becoming a man, he became a servant of God (Phil. 2:8), implying that he was not in that master-servant relationship with the Father before becoming a man. After his resurrection and ascension, Jesus continued to refer to the Father as his God (John 20:17; Rev. 3:12) and to regard the Father God as his "head" (*see* 1 Cor. 11:3).

Trinitarians have somewhat different ways of explaining these facts, but they all agree on these conclusions. *First,* the Son has always been distinct from the Father, and he always will be. *Second,* in his human nature, Christ will always honor the Father as his God. (Trinitarians believe that Jesus rose from the dead as an exalted man, not as an immaterial spirit, as the JWs teach.) *Third,* even before becoming man Christ gladly represented the Father to men and sought to honor the Father. *Fourth,* in his divine nature, Christ has always been and always will be fully God, equal to the Father in essential nature or attributes. *Fifth,* in his humanity, Christ stands in a relationship to God different than he did before becoming a man. Thus, Christ in his divine nature is *essentially* equal to the Father, though *relationally* (or functionally) subordinate or submissive to the Father, especially since becoming a man.

As we shall see, nearly all of the arguments brought against the Trinity by JWs depend to some extent on misunderstanding the Trinity.

Beyond Understanding?

To the suggestion that they do not understand the Trinity, JWs are likely to retort that no one understands it. The booklet *Should You Believe in the Trinity?* quotes from several theologians and scholarly sources to prove that even trinitarians admit that they do not understand the doctrine. The conclusion is then drawn that a doctrine that cannot be understood is not worthy of belief.

It is true that many trinitarians—Catholics especially, but also Protestants and Orthodox—state rather flatly that the Trinity cannot be understood and that it is in this sense a "mystery." The point they are making is valid, though the wording is not precise.

A "mystery" in biblical terms is generally a secret formerly unknown to man but now revealed, rather than a truth that men cannot understand. Still, these mysteries tend to have a "mysterious" element in them that cannot be completely understood by men. For example, the biblical teaching that the church is Christ's body is called a mystery (Eph. 5:32, where "mystery" appears to mean something hard to understand, as well as something that God had to reveal for us to know it).

To say that the Trinity cannot be understood likewise is imprecise, or at least open to misinterpretation. Trinitarian theologians do not mean to imply that the Trinity is unintelligible nonsense. Rather, the point they are making is that the Trinity cannot be fully fathomed, or comprehended, by the finite mind of man. There is a difference between gaining a basically correct understanding of something and having a complete, comprehensive, all-embracing, perfect understanding of it. The way many other theologians would express this difference is to say that the Trinity

can be understood, or "apprehended," but not "comprehended."

Some of the scholarly sources quoted by the JW booklet
make this very point. For example, the *Encyclopedia
Americana,* which the booklet quotes as saying that the
Trinity is "beyond the grasp of human reason," does make
that statement, but in this context:

> It is held [by trinitarians] that although the doctrine is be-
> yond the grasp of human reason, it is, like many of the
> formulations of physical science, not contrary to reason, and
> may be apprehended (though it may not be comprehended)
> by the human mind.[2]

It is therefore a mistake to argue, as JWs so often do, that
the Trinity should be rejected because it cannot be understood or because it is "confusing" (*Should You Believe in
the Trinity?,* pp. 4–5). Christians who believe in the Trinity
and have studied the doctrine carefully freely admit that
they cannot fully comprehend it, but they deny that it is
confusing. It is generally confusing only to non-Christians,
or to Christians who are new in their faith or who have
simply not taken the time to study Christian doctrine. It is
therefore unfair to reject the Trinity on the basis that "God
is not a God of confusion" (1 Cor. 14:33).

Moreover, trinitarians do not believe that it is necessary
to have a perfectly accurate understanding of the doctrine
of the Trinity as elaborated in the creeds in order to be
saved. The JWs are right when they point out that in the
Bible "common people" had faith in Jesus and knew the
truth about God. Thus, if some people find the Trinity
difficult to apprehend, they need not fear for their salvation.

The Athanasian Creed states, "We *worship* one God in
Trinity and Trinity in unity"; the emphasis is on worshiping God in keeping with truths about God that the doctrine

of the Trinity expresses, not on intellectual mastery of that doctrinal expression itself. One must worship and trust in one God, and this worship and trust must honor the Father, the Son, and the Holy Spirit as God, without either believing in three Gods or denying the clear biblical distinctions among the Father, Son, and Holy Spirit. But it is not necessary to be a theologian, or be able to understand how these things can be so, or be able to articulate the doctrine accurately, to be saved.

The purpose of careful theological formulations is not to put barriers in the way of people who are seeking salvation, but to define clearly the truths upon which genuine Christian faith rests, so that people will not be misled by false doctrines. The creeds were formulated only after certain clever people had introduced novel ways of explaining the relationships between the Father, Son, and Holy Spirit that undermined biblical faith and kept people from truly knowing God. To make clear in just what way those clever denials of the biblical teaching were wrong, it was necessary for the church to define their beliefs on these things in a formal way. Thus, while it is not necessary to understand the Trinity to be saved, or even to use the word *Trinity*, it is necessary not to reject deliberately the truths about God that the doctrine of the Trinity was formulated to express.

The Practical Significance of the Trinity

One of the complaints expressed by the JW booklet, through quotations from the *New Catholic Encyclopedia* and from Catholic theologian Joseph Bracken, is that the doctrine of the Trinity seems impractical and irrelevant, even to many people who believe in the Trinity (p. 4). It is true that in many churches today, appreciation for the Trinity is very low, even where it is formally acknowledged as true. But generally these same churches show little ap-preciation for the relevance of the Bible to their lives despite their church's official recognition of the Bible as God's Word. This is especially true in many Roman Catholic con-gregations (though not quite in all). Thus, their failure to appreciate the Trinity is no more a disproof of the truth of that doctrine than their failure to appreciate the Bible is a disproof of its truth as God's Word.

The fact is that where the Trinity is not simply given lip service, but, as the Athanasian Creed puts it, where the people "*worship* one God in Trinity," the doctrine has tremendous significance and relevance. Trinitarians have the assurance that the one who saved them, Jesus Christ, was no less than God himself. They also rejoice to know that it is God himself, in the person of the Holy Spirit, who dwells in their hearts. For the trinitarian Christian, God is not—as the JWs teach—a far-off being who sent an underling to rescue us from our sin, or who helps us now only by trans-mitting to us from far away an impersonal force or energy. Rather, God came to earth and personally saved us and is present with us directly and personally every moment. This gives the trinitarian who really believes his doctrine a tre-mendous confidence in God and an assurance that God is with him and intimately close to him.

We have here emphasized the positive significance of the doctrine of the Trinity. But the matter can be put in a different, though negative, perspective. If the Trinity is true, *creatures contribute nothing to salvation.* Jesus Christ our Savior is not a "creature," except insofar as he deigned to lower himself and share in our human nature. He is God. His death, therefore, is not a simple substitution of one perfect man for one sinful man, but the death of the God-man, a sacrifice of infinite value. Such an infinite sacri-fice for sin implies that Christ's death does not merely give men an opportunity to save themselves, but *actually* saves those who trust in him as their Savior. The Holy Spirit is not an impersonal energy that we human persons draw upon to empower ourselves; rather, the Holy Spirit *is* God, empowering us only as we live in a personal relationship with him. Thus, the doctrine of the Trinity implies that salvation is completely a work of God, from start to finish (Eph. 1:3–14; 1 Peter 1:2), and we creatures are helpless to do anything to save ourselves. Since we would like to think that we contribute something to our salvation, the Trinity is a highly offensive doctrine in that it denies us that pride. This is another reason why groups such as JWs who deny the Trinity always deny or compromise the biblical doctrines of justification through faith and salvation by grace alone.

Thus, belief in the Trinity does make a difference. It is not simply gobbledygook, a word game that has no bearing on how we view God or live our lives. Whether or not it is true can only be determined on the basis of the teaching of the Bible. But, if true, it is a teaching that persons seeking a satisfying faith should rejoice to believe.

2

▲▼▲▼▲▼▲▼▲▼▲▼▲▼▲▼▲▼▲▼▲▼▲▼▲▼▲▼

The Bible and the Trinity

Allowing the Bible the Final Word

As has just been said, the truth of the Trinity must be decided on the basis of Scripture. Here it must be confessed that not all people who believe in the Trinity are clear on this matter. Roman Catholics, in particular, often claim that the Trinity is not a biblical doctrine and was first revealed through the ministry of the church centuries after the Bible was written. This is in keeping with the Roman Catholic belief that Christian doctrine may be based either on the Bible or on church tradition (although they do insist that no doctrine may *contradict* the Bible).

Evangelical Christians, on the other hand, believe that the Bible is the only infallible source of doctrinal truth. No tradition, no religious organization, and no philosophy may add to the body of Christian doctrine, though any of these might help to explain or apply biblical doctrine. That is the perspective taken in this work.

The Word *Trinity*

It is true that the word *Trinity* is not in the Bible. However, the word *Bible* is not in the Bible, either! This is not just a cute answer with no substance. No verse in the Bible explicitly states that a certain collection of books is the only inspired writing to be recognized as God's Word. There is no list in the Bible of books that belong there—no inspired "table of contents." Yet the belief that these books, and *only* these books, belong in the Bible is itself based on the Bible's teaching, as JWs themselves recognize.

Trinitarians maintain that this is true of many biblical teachings. For example, the word *self-existent* is not in the Bible, but Christians believe that God is self-existent, that is, his existence depends on nothing outside himself. What matters is whether the ideas expressed by such words are faithful to the teaching of the Bible, not whether the words themselves can be found in its pages.

The Trinity in the Old Testament

All trinitarians agree that the ideas about God expressed in the doctrine of the Trinity are not found directly in the Old Testament. As the JW booklet notes (p. 6), some, such as Edmund Fortman, have even gone so far as to deny that the Old Testament contains "suggestions or foreshadowings or 'veiled signs' of the trinity of persons."[1] But even Fortman, on the same page as the above statement, admits that "perhaps it can be said that some of these [Old Testament] writings about word and wisdom and spirit did provide a climate in which plurality within the Godhead was conceivable to Jews."

The fact is that the Old Testament prepares for, but does not itself unfold, the revelation of God in three persons. The main burden of Old Testament revelation about God is to show forth Jehovah, the God of Israel, as the only true and living God. In a culture steeped in polytheism, it was necessary for the Israelites (who were themselves incorrigible idolaters) to have emphasized the oneness and singularity of God without qualification. Only after they were absolutely clear on this point were they at all ready to learn about the persons of the Son and the Spirit — and even then the lesson came hard to most of the Jews in the first century.

The Old Testament does contain indications that the Messiah would be God (Ps. 45:6; Isa. 7:14; 9:6) and the Son of God (Ps. 2:7). But these were not understood until after the Messiah had come.

The Trinity in the New Testament

The situation is different, however, in the New Testament. Although the New Testament does not contain a formalized explanation of the Trinity that uses such words as "Trinity," "three persons," "one substance," and the like, the ideas expressed by trinitarian language are definitely present.

The JWs, seeking to discount this claim, cite various scholarly sources (some trinitarian, some antitrinitarian) to the effect that the Trinity is not in the New Testament. For example, Fortman is quoted as stating: "The New Testament writers... give us no formal or formulated doctrine of the Trinity, no explicit teaching that in one God there are three co-equal divine persons" (p. 6). The words *formal, formulated,* and *explicit* should tip off the careful reader that Fortman is not denying that the idea of the Trinity is in the New Testament. In context, this is what Fortman actually has to say:

> If we take the New Testament writers together they tell us there is only one God, the creator and lord of the universe,

who is the Father of Jesus. They call Jesus the Son of God, Messiah, Lord, Savior, Word, Wisdom. They assign Him the divine functions of creation, salvation, judgment. Sometimes they call Him God explicitly. They do not speak as fully and clearly of the Holy Spirit as they do of the Son, but at times they coordinate Him with the Father and the Son and put Him on a level with them as far as divinity and personality are concerned. They give us in their writings a triadic ground plan and triadic formulas. They do not speak in abstract terms of nature, substance, person, relation, circumincession, mission, but they present in their own ways the ideas that are behind these terms. They give us no formal or formulated doctrine of the Trinity, no explicit teaching that in one God there are three co-equal divine persons. But they do give us an elemental trinitarianism, the data from which such a formal doctrine of the Triune God may be formulated.[2]

The JW booklet on the same page cites the *New Encyclopaedia Britannica* as saying, "Neither the word Trinity nor the explicit doctrine appears in the New Testament." Again the word *explicit* qualifies the statement. In the same paragraph the *Britannica* asserts that "the New Testament establishes the basis for the doctrine of the Trinity."[3] The same pattern is found in the citation from *The New International Dictionary of New Testament Theology:* "The N[ew] T[estament] does not contain the developed doctrine of the Trinity. 'The Bible lacks the express declaration that the Father, the Son, and the Holy Spirit are of equal essence' [said Protestant theologian Karl Barth]."[4] The words *developed* and *express* qualify the statement to allow for the presence in the New Testament of an undeveloped, implicit, and informal trinitarianism.

Also on the same page, the booklet cites E. Washburn Hopkins as stating, "To Jesus and Paul the doctrine of the trinity was apparently unknown;...they say nothing about it." This quote omits the words "at any rate" before "they say nothing about it," evidently because these words "at any rate" serve to qualify Hopkins's statement somewhat. However, even more important, in the sentence immediately preceding, Hopkins states, "The beginning of the doctrine of the trinity appears already in John (c. 100)."[5] It is clear from this statement, then, that Hopkins admitted the presence of trinitarianism in at least some portions of the New Testament.

Finally, the JW booklet cites "historian Arthur Weigall" in his book *The Paganism in Our Christianity.* It should be clear from such a title that this was no dispassionate work of scholarship, but a polemical work attacking traditional Christian beliefs.

The Trinitarian Faith of the Early Christians

What has been said above of the trinitarianism of the New Testament applies likewise to the trinitarianism of the early church. The JW booklet continues citing scholarly sources out of context to give the impression that these sources deny that the early church's faith was trinitarian.

For example, the *Encyclopaedia of Religion and Ethics* is quoted as follows: "At first the Christian faith was not Trinitarian.... It was not so in the apostolic and sub-apostolic ages, as reflected in the N[ew] T[estament] and other early Christian writings" (pp. 6–7). The first part of this quotation is cut off in mid-sentence, and reads in full, "At first the Christian faith was not Trinitarian *in the strictly ontological reference* [emphasis added]."[6] Here the point is that while the early Christians viewed God as trinitarian *economically,* in his activity in the world and in their experience, they did not explicitly speak of God as trinitarian *ontologically,* in his very essential nature or being.

But this by no means implies that the early Christians denied that this was so. Thus, the article continues on the same page, "It should be observed that there is no real cleavage or antithesis between the doctrines of the economic and the essential Trinity, and naturally so. The Tri-unity [or essential Trinity] represents the effort to think out the [economic] Trinity, and so to afford it a reasonable basis."[7] This is consistent with the article's earlier assertion that "if the doctrine of the Trinity appeared somewhat late in theology, it must have lived very early in devotion."[8]

3

▲▼▲▼▲▼▲▼▲▼▲▼▲▼▲▼▲▼▲▼▲▼▲▼▲▼▲▼▲▼▲

The Church and the Trinity

Thus far we have seen that the JWs consistently misrepresent the scholarly sources they cite in trying to prove that there is no basis in the Bible for the doctrine of the Trinity. Most of the sources they quote state that the Trinity has its basis in the New Testament, even though the formalized expressions of the doctrine were developed later.

Before turning to the biblical evidence itself—where the issue must finally be decided—the JWs also argue, again depending on a string of short quotations from scholarly sources, that the Trinity doctrine originated toward the end of the fourth century. We shall consider this claim in some detail before discussing the teaching of the Bible on the subject.

The Trinitarian Theology of the Early Fathers

The JW booklet cites selectively, and without documenting its quotations, from several Ante-Nicene Fathers (Christian writers living before the Council of Nicea) to show that none of them believed in the Trinity. These early Christian writers are quoted as if each, by being considered one of the

"Fathers," is regarded as having been completely orthodox in his theology. Such is not the case. Justin Martyr is regarded as an "apologist" in that he gave effective answers against some of the popular misconceptions of Christianity in the second century, but he is not regarded as a theologian, and he is generally criticized by Christian theologians for mixing Christian beliefs with pagan philosophy. Clement of Alexandria even more so attempted to interpret Christian beliefs in a way acceptable to pagan philosophers, and while his work is valued for some genuine insights, as a whole it has not been taken seriously since about the fourth century. Origen was in fact labeled a heretic for some of his views (though not for his views on the Trinity).

Thus, citations from the Ante-Nicene Fathers need to be treated with some caution. In many cases they reflect not the general theological beliefs of common Christians in their day, but the often brilliant, often wrongheaded, speculations of intellectuals trying to take seriously the new faith.

Nevertheless, in the main the JWs have misrepresented these Fathers, as the following survey will show.

Justin Martyr

The JW booklet *Should You Believe in the Trinity?* asserts that Justin Martyr "called the prehuman Jesus a created angel who is 'other than the God who made all things.' He said that Jesus was inferior to God and 'never did anything except what the Creator... willed him to do and say'" (p. 7).

The fact is that Justin Martyr taught that the prehuman Jesus was God, not an angel. Justin did say that Christ was called an angel, but explained that this was because Christ, who was actually God, took on the appearance of an angel. Thus, Justin writes that "the Father of the universe has a

Son; who also, being the first-begotten Word of God, *is even God*. And of old he appeared in the shape of fire and in the likeness of an angel to Moses and to the other prophets... [emphasis added]."[1] Elsewhere, Justin calls Christ "both God and Lord of hosts" (that is, Jehovah),[2] "God the Son of God."[3]

Justin not only believed that Christ was God; he believed in a rudimentary form of the Trinity. Thus, he stated that Christians worshiped God the Father, "the Son (who came forth from Him...), and the prophetic Spirit."[4] That this meant that Christ and the Spirit were both God is implied by his repeated statement that "we ought to worship God alone... to God alone we render worship."[5]

In short, although Justin Martyr did not use such terms as "Trinity," and his philosophical explanations of the relation of Christ to God were somewhat confused, he worshiped Father, Son, and Holy Spirit, and he regarded Christ as Jehovah God.

Irenaeus

The Watchtower booklet says that Irenaeus, a late-second-century theologian, held that Christ was inferior to God, "not equal to the 'One true and only God,' who is 'supreme over all, and besides whom there is no other'" (p. 7). But in context Irenaeus was contrasting the "one true and only God" with the lesser gods of Gnostic speculation (about which more will be said later), not denying that Christ is God.

In fact, Irenaeus defended a view of the Father, Son, and Holy Spirit that was implicitly trinitarian. Thus, he states that the church has its faith "in one God, the Father Almighty, Maker of heaven, and earth, and the sea, and all things that are in them; and in one Christ Jesus, the Son of God, who became incarnate for our salvation; and in the

Holy Spirit, who proclaimed through the prophets the dispensations of God," and in the same context speaks of "Christ Jesus, our Lord, and God, and Saviour, and King."[6] Irenaeus writes of "Christ Jesus, the Son of God; who, because of his surpassing love towards *His creation*, condescended to be born of the virgin, He Himself uniting man through Himself to God... [emphasis added]."[7] Thus Jesus Christ was both God and man, the Creator who became a man to save his creation.

Clement of Alexandria

The JW booklet claims that Clement of Alexandria held that Christ was "a creature" and inferior to God (p. 7). In fact, Clement held the opposite. He taught that Christ is "truly most manifest Deity, He that is made equal to the Lord of the universe; because He was His Son,"[8] and one and the same God as the Father.[9] Clement explicitly called Christ the "eternal Son,"[10] and denied that the Father had ever been without the Son.[11]

Tertullian

Tertullian not only believed in the Trinity, he formulated the basic terminology used in formal expressions of the doctrine. The word *Trinity*, as well as the distinction between "one God" and "three persons," was first developed by Tertullian. He wrote explicitly of "a trinity of one divinity, Father, Son and Holy Spirit."[12]

The JW booklet cites Tertullian as saying, "The Father is different from the Son (another), as he is greater; as he who begets is different from him who is begotten; he who sends, different from he who is sent" (p. 7). This is classic trinitarianism. Tertullian's point was that the Father and the Son were distinct persons. As was pointed out in our discussion of the meaning of the Trinity, JWs commonly misunderstand the Trinity to teach that the Father is the Son.

The booklet also quotes Tertullian as saying, "There was a time when the Son was not.... Before all things, God was alone." Actually, the expression "there was a time when the Son was not" was not used by Tertullian himself. Rather, this was an expression used by a modern scholar to summarize a statement made by Tertullian,[13] who argued that God was always God, but not always Father of the Son: "For He could not have been the Father previous to the Son, nor a judge previous to sin."[14] Since elsewhere Tertullian makes clear that he regards the *person* of the Son as eternal, in this statement Tertullian is probably asserting that the title of "Son" did not apply to the second person of the Trinity until he began to relate to the "Father" as a "Son" in the work of creation.[15]

The statement "Before all things, God was alone," appears in an entirely different work by Tertullian, in which he states that the "Reason" of God was the Word prior to his activity in creation, and thus that this person called Reason existed eternally alongside God: "For before all things God was alone.... Yet even not then was He alone; for He had with Him that which He possessed in Himself, that is to say, His own Reason.... Even then before the creation of the universe God was not alone, since He had within Himself both Reason, and, inherent in Reason, His Word...."[16] This Word is the Son, equal to God, yet second to the Father functionally: "Thus does He [the Father] make Him [the Son] *equal to Him.* . . . while I recognize the Son, I assert His distinction as second to the Father [emphasis added]."[17]

Thus, although his language was sometimes inconsistent, Tertullian clearly believed in the Trinity. In a desperate attempt to deny this fact, the JW booklet states:

However, this [the use of the word *trinitas* by Tertullian] is no proof in itself that Tertullian taught the Trinity. The Catholic work *Trinitas—A Theological Encyclopedia of the*

Holy Trinity, for example, notes that some of Tertullian's words were later used by others to describe the Trinity. Then it cautions: "But hasty conclusions cannot be drawn from usage, for he does not apply the words to Trinitarian theology" [*Should You Believe in the Trinity?*, 5–6].

One would assume from this argument that the Catholic work *Trinitas* is saying that Tertullian did not use the word *trinitas* ("Trinity") of God in a trinitarian context. But this is absolutely false. In fact, the encyclopedia is saying that Tertullian did not use the *substantia* word group with reference to the Trinity. Note what the work actually says:

The great African fashioned the Latin language of the Trinity, and many of his words and phrases remained permanently in use: the words *Trinitas* and *persona*, the formulas "one substance in three persons," "God from God, Light from Light." He uses the word *substantia* 400 times, as he uses *consubstantialis* and *consubstantivus*, but hasty conclusions cannot be drawn from usage, for he does not apply the words to Trinitarian theology.[18]

One can only conclude that the writer or writers of the JW booklet were hard-pressed to find solid evidence for their belief that the Trinity was developed almost two centuries after Tertullian.

Hippolytus

The Watchtower booklet quotes Hippolytus as saying that God was "alone by himself" and "called into being what had no being before." This agrees fully with trinitarian belief. But then the booklet says that Hippolytus included among those things God called into being "the created prehuman Jesus" (p. 7). This is not only incorrect, but it flatly contradicts Hippolytus's own teaching in the very context in which he made these statements.

Hippolytus writes: "God, subsisting alone, and having nothing contemporaneous with Himself, determined to create the world.... there was nothing contemporaneous with God. Beside Him there was nothing; *but He, while existing alone, yet existed in plurality* [emphasis added]."[19]

This plurality consists of the Father, Son, and Holy Spirit, as Hippolytus states in a preceding paragraph:

> A man, therefore, even though he will it not, is compelled to acknowledge God the Father Almighty, and Christ Jesus the Son of God, who, being God, became man, to whom also the Father made all things subject, Himself excepted, and the Holy Spirit; and that these, therefore, are three.[20]

Hippolytus even states that Scripture calls "Christ the Almighty"[21] and that "Christ is the God above all."[22] It is therefore undeniable that the JWs have misrepresented the teaching of Hippolytus.

Origen

Origen, as previously mentioned, was eventually to be regarded as a heretic. Although the cause for this judgment was not his teaching on the Trinity, the church has always regarded Origen's way of explaining the Trinity to be very helpful in some respects and flat wrong in others.

On the one hand, Origen clearly believed in some form of the Trinity. Edmund J. Fortman demonstrates this fact with several brief quotations from Origen:

> "We, however, are persuaded that there are really three persons [*treis hypostaseis*], the Father, the Son and the Holy Spirit" (*Jo.* 2.6). For him "statements made regarding Father, Son and Holy Spirit are to be understood as transcending all time, all ages, and all eternity" (*Princ.* 4.28), and there is "nothing which was not made, save the nature of the Father, and the Son, and the Holy Spirit" (*Princ.* 4.35).

"Moreover, nothing in the Trinity can be called greater or less" (*Princ.* 1.3.7).[23]

On the other hand, Origen was unorthodox in other aspects of his teaching on the Trinity. He tended to view the three persons more or less as three Gods, though without ever putting it just so, and (inconsistently) held that the Son and Spirit, though far superior beings to any creatures, were inferior to the Father. He thus also denied that worship or prayer should be addressed to the Son or the Spirit.[24]

In sum, Origen's view of God had similarities both to orthodox trinitarianism and to the JWs' doctrine of God. Unlike the Witnesses, Origen believed that the Son was eternal and uncreated, and he definitely regarded the Spirit as a person. But, like the Witnesses, he regarded the Son as a second, inferior God next to Almighty God.

Assessing the Ante-Nicene Fathers

The teaching of the Ante-Nicene Fathers is generally trinitarian. This is implicit in the second-century Fathers (Justin Martyr, Irenaeus, Clement of Alexandria) and becomes fairly explicit in the third-century Fathers (Tertullian, Hippolytus, Origen). The Ante-Nicene Fathers who exerted the most influence on the trinitarian language of the church after Nicea were Tertullian and Origen. Of these two thinkers, the summary judgment of Gerald Bray is to the point: "Tertullian's theology, despite its lapses, was fundamentally sound and later orthodoxy did little more than tidy up loose ends in his work. Origen, on the other hand, has been completely reworked. His contribution remains, but it has been given a new context and a different meaning."[25]

Where the Ante-Nicene Fathers departed from trinitarianism was largely in their attempts to *explain* the Trinity in terms that would be understandable and acceptable to

Jews (Justin Martyr) and to pagans (Justin again, Clement, Origen). Their tendencies toward subordinationism and tritheism were at odds with their own statements about the church's common faith in and worship of the Father, Son, and Holy Spirit.

Early Nontrinitarian Theologies

In order to evaluate properly the JW claim that the doctrine of the Trinity was a departure from the early Christian faith, it is necessary to say something about the early heresies. These were nontrinitarian, alternative forms of Christianity that the church fathers rejected and that forced the church to define its trinitarian faith more precisely.

Gnosticism

Since the subject of *Gnosticism* is very complex, it will be necessary to oversimplify somewhat. Gnosticism was not one religious sect or teaching, but a widespread movement that took many forms, some purporting to be Christian and some not. The essential idea of Gnosticism was that man was a divine spirit trapped in a corrupt material world and in need of a special "knowledge" *(gnosis)* in order to escape this material world. Gnostics of a "Christian" bent held that the supreme God had emanated lesser gods, including one who created the material world and trapped our spirits in it. They further held that "the Christ" was a good divine being, working to undo the damage done by the evil creator-god. This Christ came on the man Jesus temporarily and abandoned him just before his death.

JWs should have no trouble seeing that this theory was completely false and unbiblical. The second-century church fathers considered Gnosticism to be heretical, and in their writings emphasized that the supreme God was also the Creator and that there was no disunity of mind or purpose among the Father, Son, and Holy Spirit.

Monarchianism

The term *Monarchianism* is sometimes used as a catch-all for a number of theories that surfaced beginning around the end of the second century. According to these theories, the supreme God was one person, the Father, and had manifested himself in Jesus. One version of this idea, *Modalism,* held that the Father, Son, and Holy Spirit were three successive "modes" in which the one God manifested himself and worked to bring salvation to the world. Other versions held (or were said by the orthodox to imply) that the Father was made flesh, died, and rose from the dead.

The JWs will easily recognize this view as unbiblical. What they may not so easily recognize is that it was not trinitarian. The leading church fathers of the third century all regarded these views as heretical. Trinitarians recognize that the Son is a person distinct from the Father and deny that the Father became flesh.

Arianism

Arianism arose in the early fourth century through the teaching of Arius of Alexandria. Arius, claiming to follow in the footsteps of the second-century Alexandrian church father Origen, held that the Son was a second God, inferior to the Father, and that the Holy Spirit was a third God, inferior to both the Father and the Son. Unlike Origen, however, Arius denied that the Son and the Holy Spirit were eternal, maintaining that "there was a time when the Son was not" and describing both the Son and the Holy Spirit as exalted creatures.

Of all the alternative views to trinitarianism that circulated in the first three centuries after the apostolic era,

Arianism seems closest to the view of the JWs. The main doctrinal difference seems to be that the Arians regarded the Holy Spirit as a personal being, whereas the Witnesses teach that "holy spirit" is an impersonal energy or force emitted by God.

However, it is interesting to note that JWs today do not claim that the Arians were their ancient counterparts. There is good reason for this, other than the disagreement over the Holy Spirit. Historically, there is no doubt that Arius's views were a novelty. He was not part of a fellowship of believers who regarded themselves as the faithful Christians and the trinitarians as apostates. While he built on Origen's ideas, Arius also disagreed sharply with them, and in a way that no one in the church had imagined before.

Where Were the Jehovah's Witnesses?

All this raises an interesting question. Where, during the centuries following the New Testament era, were the ancient counterparts to today's JWs? According to the Witnesses, the church fell into apostasy sometime after the apostolic era, and the truths of the Bible were restored only in the late-nineteenth and early-twentieth centuries in their religion. If this is so, we would expect to find some record of a religious group in the second or third century with views resembling at least somewhat those of the JWs. But such is not the case. The closest parallel is the Arian movement, but it did not exist until the fourth century.

Constantine and Nicea

The JW booklet contains a number of false or misleading assertions regarding the Council of Nicea and the Roman emperor Constantine's role in it. The booklet states that the council "did not establish the doctrine of the Trinity, for at that council there was no mention of the holy spirit as the third person of a triune Godhead" (p. 7). While the council did not define its view of the Holy Spirit, the Creed of Nicea (not to be confused with the later work popularly known as the Nicene Creed) was trinitarian in structure: "We believe in one God the Father.... And in one Lord Jesus Christ.... And in the Holy Spirit."[26] Nothing was said about the Holy Spirit simply because the subject of controversy was the person of the Son. Thus, the council upheld a trinitarian theology without elaborating on the person of the Holy Spirit.

The booklet then claims that "for many years, there had been much opposition on Biblical grounds to the developing idea that Jesus was God" (p. 8). Actually, as we have seen, this was the view of the church from the second century on (at least), and the only dissenters were heretics whom even the JWs would regard as non-Christians.

Next we are told that only "a fraction of the total" number of bishops attended the Council of Nicea. Since this might be taken to imply that the council was stacked in favor of the trinitarians, it should be pointed out that precisely the opposite was the case. Most of the bishops were from the East, where most of the Arians were found; very few bishops came from the West, although the West was solidly trinitarian.[27]

The booklet then repeats the conventional view that Constantine was not a sincere Christian, but a mere pagan using Christianity for political purposes. This is false, as has been well explained in *The New Encyclopaedia Britannica:*

> Constantine's personal "theology" emerges with particular clarity from a remarkable series of letters, extending from 313 to the early 320s, concerning the Donatist schism in North Africa.... Schism, in Constantine's view, was "insane, futile madness," inspired by the Devil, the author of evil. Its

partisans were acting in defiance of the clemency of Christ, for which they might expect eternal damnation at the Last Judgment (this was a Judgment whose rigours Constantine equally anticipated for himself). Meanwhile, it was for the righteous members of the Christian community to show patience and longsuffering. In so doing they would be imitating Christ and their patience would be rewarded in lieu of martyrdom.... Throughout, Constantine had no doubt whatever that to remove error and propagate the true religion was both his personal duty and a proper use of the imperial position.

Such pronouncements, expressed in letters to imperial officials and to Christian clergy, make untenable the view that Constantine's religious attitudes were even in these early years either veiled, confused, or compromised. Openly expressed, his attitudes show a clear commitment.[28]

The Watchtower booklet next quotes the *Encyclopaedia Britannica* (an earlier edition) as relating that Constantine "personally proposed... the crucial formula expressing the relation of Christ to God in the creed issued by the council, 'of one substance with the Father.'" What is omitted here is that Constantine made this proposal probably at the suggestion of his theological adviser, Hosius, a bishop from Spain. Moreover, the idea expressed by the term was not new.

The booklet then concludes that Constantine "intervened and decided in favor of those who said that Jesus was God." This is simply false. What Constantine did was to encourage the bishops to reach as near a consensus as possible and then used his political authority to depose those few bishops who insisted on opposing that consensus. The vast majority of the bishops firmly believed that Jesus is God; had they not, it would have been counterproductive to Constantine's purpose to decide "in favor of those who said that Jesus was God."

The actual creed adopted by the council, drawn up by Eusebius of Caesarea, described Christ as "God of God," even before Constantine's suggestion of the expression "of one substance with the Father." Before this creed was drawn up and accepted, another creed drawn up by Eusebius of Nicomedia, an Arian, was considered. Even though most of the council bishops were from the East and there were more committed Arians than trinitarians, the council "roundly rejected" the Arian creed because it denied that Jesus was God.[29] As for the trinitarian creed, the only part of it with which many of the Eastern bishops were uncomfortable was the expression "of one substance with the Father." The reason was not because it implied that Jesus was God (which most of them took for granted) or because it was trinitarian, but because it sounded to them too much like Monarchianism.

After Nicea

Although Constantine backed the trinitarians at Nicea, that was not the end of the Arian controversy. The JW booklet understates the case when it admits, "Those who believed that Jesus was not equal to God even came back into favor for a time." In fact, Constantine reversed himself in A.D. 332, seven years after the Council of Nicea, and supported Arius. For 45 of the next 49 years the Arians were in favor with the Roman emperors.[30] For much of this time Athanasius, one of the leading trinitarians at Nicea, was practically the only Christian leader who was unwilling to compromise with the Arians, giving rise to the saying *Athanasius contra mundum,* "Athanasius against the world." But in 381 the emperor Theodosius, who held to the Trinity, declared trinitarian Christianity the official religion of the empire and convened the Council of Constantinople, where an even more explicit trinitarian creed was adopted.

Many people, including the JWs, express offense at the establishment of trinitarianism by the Roman Empire as its official religion. Does this not imply that the doctrine of the Trinity was somehow more pagan than Christian, and that it was accepted by the masses only because it was the emperor's command?

The answer to this question is decidedly no. During the height of the Arian controversy between 325 and 381, Arianism was generally recognized by the emperors as a more attractive religious system than trinitarianism. The reason this was so is that Arianism, which taught that Jesus was a divine creature, implied that a creature could be a God, could become highly exalted and command unconditional allegiance from men. That was an attractive idea to the emperors, whose pagan predecessors often demanded worship, and who found it easier to rule if the people thought of them as in some sense divine. Trinitarianism, on the other hand, held all divinity to be possessed by the triune God and maintained a sharper distinction between the Creator and the creature; as such, it implied that the emperor was just an ordinary man.[31] That a Roman emperor would declare trinitarian Christianity to be his empire's official religion is therefore surprising and suggests that concern for truth won out over political expediency.

However much the triumph of trinitarianism owed to the political support of the empire, the question of the truth or falsehood of the Trinity cannot be decided by its political fortunes. It is simply faulty reasoning to assume that whatever belief is supported by political leaders must be false. The leading champions of trinitarianism, especially Athanasius, were careful interpreters of the Bible and passionately committed to Jesus Christ as their God and Savior.

Finally, it should be noted that the Watchtower booklet's claim that "even after the Council of Constantinople, the Trinity did not become a widely accepted creed," is false. While Arianism did not disappear at that time, the Trinity enjoyed widespread acceptance; in fact it had been the majority viewpoint of professing Christians for centuries earlier. Further developments in trinitarian theology were simply refinements on relatively minor points. While the Athanasian Creed was not written by Athanasius, it was faithful to the theology of Athanasius and was simply a more explicit affirmation and precise formulation of what the church had already believed.

Pagan Beliefs and the Christian Trinity

Antitrinitarians during the past three centuries have commonly maintained that the Trinity was borrowed from pagan beliefs. It is possible to quote from many scholarly and not-so-scholarly sources to this effect. The JW booklet quotes a number of sources that argue, or in some cases seem to imply, that the Trinity was a pagan notion that corrupted the Christian faith (pp. 9, 11–12). It also reproduces pictures of various pagan "triads," or groups of three gods, and places them alongside pictures of Christian artwork depicting or symbolizing the Trinity (pp. 2, 10).

There are a number of problems with this argument. First, at least some of the sources quoted by the booklet have been misrepresented. For example, the *Encyclopaedia of Religion and Ethics* is quoted in its descriptions of some "trinitarian" parallels in Egyptian religion and Neoplatonic philosophy. But in context the encyclopedia is discussing similar notions, not identifying sources or influences of the Christian Trinity. On the same page this work states, "This Christian faith in the incarnation of the divine

Word *(logos, sermo, ratio)* in the man Christ Jesus, with whom the believer is united through the fellowship of the Holy Spirit, constitutes the distinctive basis of the Christian doctrine of the Trinity."[32]

Second, the booklet does not point to one or two sources for the doctrine of the Trinity and explain how they influenced its development. Instead, it quotes from a variety of works claiming that several widely different pagan notions paralleled or may have been sources for the Trinity. Egyptian, Babylonian, Assyrian, Hindu, and Buddhist triads, as well as Platonism, are all claimed as influencing the development of the Trinity. But it is absurd to claim that all of these significantly influenced the trinitarians.

Third, most of these alleged "influences" were either far too early or far too late, or far too removed geographically, to have any significant influence. Artwork picturing Egyptian and Babylonian triads are reproduced, despite the fact that the art dated from about two thousand years before the Witnesses claim the Trinity originated! Other artwork depicting Hindu and Buddhist triads from the seventh and twelfth centuries are shown, despite the fact that these were done centuries after the Trinity had become the official religion of the Roman Empire!

Fourth, the JW booklet points out that Athanasius was a bishop in Alexandria, Egypt, and from this fact argues that his trinitarianism reflected the influence of Egyptian triads (p. 11). But this geographical coincidence is no more significant than the fact that Athanasius's archrival, Arius, was also from Alexandria!

Fifth, while it is true that pagan peoples of the ancient world worshiped triads of gods, these triads were always three separate gods, not one God. Moreover, they were always or nearly always merely the three gods at the top of the hierarchy of many gods worshiped in polytheistic religions.

Sixth, a comparison of trinitarianism with the major non-trinitarian heresies of the early centuries shows that they, not the Trinity, were corruptions due to the influence of paganism, and especially of Neoplatonism. For example, the "Christian" Gnostics held to the Neoplatonic idea that the spiritual was good and the material was evil. Consequently, the supreme and perfectly spiritual God could not have created the world himself, and therefore it must have been made by some inferior deity. Arianism betrays a similar thinking in its teaching that God did not make the material world, but rather made the Word and allowed the Word, an inferior deity, to make the world. In opposition to these theories, trinitarians upheld the biblical teaching that God alone is the Creator and Maker of all things (Gen. 1:1; Isa. 44:24).

Gnosticism, Monarchianism, and Arianism also all agreed that the Supreme Being must be an undifferentiated One. That is—in keeping with the Neoplatonic idea that the One is completely separate from the many, free of all plurality—they found it unthinkable that God should be three in any sense. Thus, the Gnostics and the Arians held that Jesus was a separate divinity from the supreme God, and the Monarchians held that Jesus was a manifestation of the Father, the only divine person. Despite their differences, therefore, all of these heresies assumed that God could not be one in one sense and three in another sense. This assumption was inherited from pagan philosophy, not from the Bible, which simply states that God is one without ever denying that God is in another sense three. On the other hand, the trinitarians insisted that the issue of God's oneness and threeness had to be decided on the basis of the Bible alone, without importing alien assumptions from Greek philosophy.

Thus, the historical facts show that trinitarianism developed its precise theological formulas and creeds, not to baptize paganism into Christianity, but to safeguard biblical truths from corruption by paganism.

What Is the Apostasy?

According to the Witnesses, the development of trinitarian theology matches the New Testament predictions concerning "an apostasy, a deviation, a falling away from true worship until Christ's return" (p. 9); the JWs believe "Christ's return" took place figuratively in A.D. 1914. They argue that trinitarianism fulfilled this prediction by mixing pagan religion and philosophy with Christianity.

As we have seen, the historical facts regarding the development of the doctrine of the Trinity do not support the JWs' contention. Trinitarianism represented the triumph of biblical monotheism and the revelation of God in Christ over pagan polytheism.

There are better ways of interpreting the references to apostasy in the New Testament. For one thing, some of the references to false doctrine and apostasy that the Witnesses cite probably apply to different heresies and different periods of church history. Certainly some of the biblical warnings about heresy were fulfilled to some extent (if not completely) long before the fourth century.

For instance, one of the passages referenced as speaking of "the apostasy" warned of persons who denied that Jesus Christ had come in the flesh (1 John 4:1–3). This was fulfilled in Gnostic speculations that Christ was a divine spirit that rested on Jesus without actually becoming man. These notions were in full flower in the second century, and many of the early church theologians wrote works refuting them.

Another passage cited by the Witness booklet warns of a "man of lawlessness" who seats himself in the temple of

God and claims to be God (2 Thess. 2:3–7). Whatever this prophecy means—and it has been interpreted in a dizzying variety of ways—there would not appear to be anything about the events of the fourth century or the development of trinitarianism that might be connected to the prophecy.

If the prediction of an apostasy has reference to a massive turning away from the truth by a large portion of the professing Christian church, the so-called Enlightenment stands out as the best candidate so far in recorded history. In the sixteenth and seventeenth centuries nearly all of the professing Christian culture was experiencing renewed faith in Christ and in the Bible as God's Word. Yet, in the eighteenth and nineteenth centuries, this same culture largely abandoned even a profession of that faith as critical theories about the Bible's origin, skeptical denials of miracles, and the theory of naturalistic evolution changed the dominant world view of the West from Christian to secular.

Also during this period, and continuing into the twentieth century, a large number of alternative versions of Christian religion came into being. Most of these religions originated in the northeastern United States and were founded by former Protestants. These religions included Unitarianism, Mormonism, New Thought, Christian Science, Unity School of Christianity, Theosophy (which is one of the principal sources of the contemporary New Age movement), modern spiritism (another major precursor to the New Age movement)—and Jehovah's Witnesses.

The JWs will no doubt be offended to be included in such a list, and there are, of course, differences among these various religions. But all of them have in common, besides their time and place of origin, a firm belief inherited from the Enlightenment that the orthodox Christianity of the previous fifteen centuries was no longer acceptable. In particular, all of them reject the Trinity.

Whether or not antitrinitarianism is an aspect of "the apostasy," it certainly cannot be denied that the JWs' rejection of the Trinity is consistent with the spirit of the times. Followers of humanism, secularism, theological liberalism, New Age philosophies, and pseudo-Christian sects all agree that the Trinity is no longer believable. This does not in isolation prove that the Trinity *is* true, of course, but it ought at least to warn JWs that denying the Trinity is no sign of insight into truth.

4

▲▼▲▼▲▼▲▼▲▼▲▼▲▼▲▼▲▼▲▼▲▼▲▼▲▼▲

Will the Real Polytheists
Please Stand Up?

The rest of this book will be concerned with the biblical material relating to the Trinity, considering the arguments advanced by JWs to show that it is unbiblical.

We begin with the biblical teaching that there is one God. The JWs affirm that monotheism is the biblical teaching (p. 12), citing several Scriptures in support (p. 13). And trinitarians could not agree more. There is only one God, and this God is one. The oneness of God is the first plank in the trinitarian platform. For this reason I would agree with the booklet's argument that the plural form *elohim* for God in the Old Testament cannot be evidence of the Trinity (pp. 13–14).

The Trinity and the Oneness of God

But two problems need attention. First, JWs claim that the Bible's affirmations of monotheism mean "that God is one Person—a unique, unpartitioned Being who has no equal" (p. 13). As has already been explained, trinitarians do not regard the three persons as "partitions" of God, or the Son and Spirit as beings outside God yet equal to him. Indeed, if "person" is defined to mean an individual personal being, then trinitarians will agree that *in that sense* "God is one Person." Thus, in arguing as if these truths contradicted the Trinity, the JWs show they have misconstrued the doctrine. In fact, that God is one "Person" in this sense does not prove that he is not also three "persons" in the sense meant by trinitarians.

Second, biblical monotheism does not simply mean that the being of the Almighty God is one being. That is true enough, but the Bible also teaches simply that there is one God. The Bible is quite emphatic on this point, repeating it often in both the Old Testament (Deut. 4:35, 39; 32:39; 2 Sam. 22:32; Isa. 37:20; 43:10; 44:6–8; 45:5, 14, 21–22; 46:9) and the New Testament (Rom. 3:30; 16:27; 1 Cor. 8:4, 6; Gal. 3:20; Eph. 4:6; 1 Tim. 1:17; 2:5; James 2:19; Jude 25). And the very meaning of the word *monotheism* is the belief in one God.

It is therefore important to note that the JWs flatly deny this most basic of biblical teachings. Although they admit that there is only one *Almighty* God, they claim that there are, in addition to that God, and not counting the many false gods worshiped by idolaters, many creatures rightly recognized in the Bible as "gods" in the sense of "mighty ones" (p. 28). These "gods" include Jesus Christ, angels, human judges, and Satan. The JWs take this position to justify allowing the Bible to call Jesus "a god" without honoring him as Jehovah God.

The question must therefore be asked whether Witnesses can escape the charge that they are polytheists (believers in many gods). The usual reply is that while they believe there are many gods, they *worship* only one God, Jehovah. But this belief is not monotheism, either. The usual term for the belief that there are many gods but only one who is to be worshiped is *henotheism*.

The more important question, of course, is whether the Bible supports the JWs' view. The explicit, direct statements of the Bible that there is only one God (cited above) cannot fairly be interpreted to mean that there are many gods but only one who is almighty, or only one who is to be worshiped, or only one who is named Jehovah. There *is* only one Almighty God Jehovah, and he alone is to be worshiped—but the Bible also states flatly that he is the only God.

More precisely, the Bible says that there is only one *true God* (John 17:3; *see also* 2 Chron. 15:3; Jer. 10:10; 1 Thess. 1:9; 1 John 5:20), in contrast to all other gods, *false gods*, who are not gods at all (Deut. 32:21; 1 Sam. 12:21; Ps. 96:5; Isa. 37:19; 41:23–24, 29; Jer. 2:11; 5:7; 16:20; 1 Cor. 8:4; 10:19–20). There are, then, two categories of "gods": true Gods (of which there is only one, Jehovah) and false gods (of which there are unfortunately many).

The JWs, however, in agreement with most antitrinitarian groups today that claim to believe in the Bible, cannot agree that there is only one true God, despite the Bible's saying so in just those words, because then they would have to admit that Jesus is that God. Therefore, they appeal to a few isolated texts in the Bible that they claim honor creatures with the title *gods* without implying that they are false gods. We must next consider these texts briefly.

Are Angels Gods?

There are two kinds of creatures that the JWs claim are honored as gods in Scripture—angels and men. We begin with angels. The usual prooftext in support of this claim is Psalm 8:5, which the NWT renders, "You also proceeded to make him [man] a little less than godlike ones." The word translated "godlike ones" here is *elohim*, the usual word for "God," but (because plural) also translatable as "gods." Since Hebrews 2:7 quotes this verse as saying, "You made him a little lower than *angels*" (NWT), the Witnesses conclude that Psalm 8:5 is calling angels "gods."

There are numerous objections to this line of reasoning, only some of which can be mentioned here. First, it is questionable that in its original context *elohim* in Psalm 8:5 should be understood to refer to angels and translated "gods" or "godlike ones." This is because in context this psalm is speaking of man's place in creation in terms that closely parallel Genesis 1. Psalm 8:3 speaks of the creation of the heavens, moon, and stars (cf. Gen. 1:1, 8, 16). Verse 4 asks how God can consider man significant when compared with the grandeur of creation. The answer given is that man rules over creation—over the inhabitants of the land, sky, and sea (vv. 6–8; cf. Gen. 1:26–28). What links this question and answer in Psalm 8 is the statement that God made man "a little lower than *elohim*," which parallels in thought the Genesis statement that man was created "in the image of *elohim*," that is, in the image of God (Gen. 1:26–27). This makes it quite reasonable to conclude that in its own context Psalm 8:5 is meant to be understood as saying that man is a little lower than God, not angels.

If this view is correct, why does Hebrews 2:7 have the word *angels* rather than *God?* The simple answer is that the author of Hebrews was quoting from the Septuagint, a Greek translation of the Old Testament prepared by Jewish scholars and in common use in the first century. The fact that the writer of Hebrews quoted the Septuagint does not imply that the Septuagint rendering he quoted was a literal or accurate word-for-word translation of the Hebrew text (after all, "angels" is certainly not a literal translation of "gods"). Rather, Hebrews 2:7 is a paraphrase of Psalm 8:5

that, while introducing a new understanding of it, does not contradict it. Psalm 8 says that the son of man (meaning mankind) was made a little lower than God; Hebrews 2 says that the Son of Man (meaning Christ) was made a little lower than the angels. The psalm speaks of man's exalted status, while Hebrews speaks of Christ's temporary humbling. Since the angels are, of course, lower than God, and since Christ's humbled status was that of a man, what Hebrews says does not contradict Psalm 8:5, though it does go beyond it.

It must be admitted that this is not the only way of reading Hebrews 2:7 and Psalm 8:5. It is just possible that Hebrews 2:7 does implicitly understand Psalm 8:5 to be calling angels "gods." If this were correct, it would not mean that angels were *truly* gods. It might then be argued that the point of Psalm 8:5 was that man was made just a little lower than the spiritual creatures so often wrongly worshiped by men as gods. This would fit the context of Hebrews 2:7 also, since from Hebrews 1:5 through the end of chapter 2 the author argues for the superiority of the Son over angels. That is, Hebrews might be taken to imply that even God's angels can be idolized if they are wrongly exalted or worshiped as gods (which some early heretics were doing [cf. Col. 2:18]).

Moreover, this interpretation would also fit Hebrews 1:6, which quotes Psalm 97:7 as saying that all of God's angels should worship the Son. Psalm 97:7 in Hebrew is a command to the "gods" (identified in the immediate context as *idols*) to *worship Jehovah*. Thus, Hebrews 1:6 testifies at once both to the fact that angels, if they are considered gods at all, are false gods, and that Jesus Christ is worshiped by angels as Jehovah the true God.

There are other reasons for denying that angels are truly gods in a positive sense. The Bible flatly states that demonic spirits are not gods (1 Cor. 10:20; Gal. 4:8). Since demons are just as much spirits, and presumably are just as much "mighty ones" (though wicked) as the holy angels, it follows that angels cannot be gods by virtue of their being "mighty ones."

Furthermore, the translation of *elohim* in Psalm 8:5 as "godlike ones" runs into the problem of contradicting the Bible, which flatly and repeatedly states that none are like God (Exod. 8:10; 9:14; 15:11; 2 Sam. 7:22; 1 Kings 8:23; 1 Chron. 17:20; Ps. 86:8; Isa. 40:18, 25; 44:7; 46:5, 9; Jer. 10:6–7; Mic. 7:18), though creatures may reflect God's moral qualities (Rom. 8:29; Eph. 4:24; Col. 3:10; 2 Peter 1:4; 1 John 3:2).

Finally, even if angels *were* gods in some positive sense, that would not explain in what sense Jesus Christ is called "God," since he is not an angel—he is God's Son (Heb. 1:4–5); is worshiped by all the angels (Heb. 1:6); is the God who reigns, not a spirit messenger (Heb. 1:7–9); and is the Lord who created everything, not an angel created to serve (Heb. 1:10–13).

Before leaving this question, it should be noted in passing that Satan is called "the god of this age" (2 Cor. 4:4 NIV), but clearly in the sense of a false god, one who is wrongly allowed to usurp the place of the true God in the present age. That is the point of 2 Corinthians 4:4, not that Satan is a mighty one.

Are Mighty Men Gods?

The Witnesses claim that not only mighty angels, but also mighty men, are called "gods" in Scripture in recognition of their might. This claim, however, is open to even more difficult objections than the claim that angels are gods.

The Bible explicitly denies that powerful men, such as kings and dictators and military leaders, are gods (Ezek. 28:2, 9; *see also* Isa. 31:3; 2 Thess. 2:4). In fact, frequently in Scripture "man" and "God" are used as opposite categories, parallel with "flesh" and "spirit" (Num. 23:19; Isa. 31:3; Hos. 11:9; Matt. 19:26; John 10:33; Acts 12:22; 1 Cor. 14:2). In this light, texts that are alleged to call men "gods" in a positive sense ought to be studied carefully and alternative interpretations followed where context permits.

The usual text cited in this connection, as in the JW booklet, is Psalm 82:6, "I said, you are gods," which is quoted by Jesus in John 10:34. This verse has commonly been interpreted (by trinitarians as well as antitrinitarians, though with different conclusions drawn) to be calling Israelite judges "gods" by virtue of their honorable office of representing God to the people in judgment. Assuming this interpretation to be correct, the verse would not then be saying that judges really are gods in the sense of "mighty ones." Rather, it would simply be saying that as judges in Israel they represented God. This *representative* sense of "gods" would then have to be distinguished from a *qualitative* sense, in which creatures are called "gods" as a description of the kind of beings they are.

There are good reasons, however, to think that the Israelite judges are being called "gods" not to honor them but to expose them as false gods. This may be seen best by a close reading of the entire psalm.

In Psalm 82:1 Jehovah God is spoken of by the psalmist in the third person: "God takes His stand... He judges..." (NASB). The psalmist says, "God *[elohim]* takes his stand in the assembly of God *[el]*; he judges in the midst of the gods *[elohim]*" (my translation). Here we are confronted with two *elohim*: God, and the judges, called by the psalmist "gods."

In verses 2–5 God's judgment against the Israelite judges is pronounced. They are unjust, show partiality to the wicked, allow the wicked to abuse the poor and helpless, and by their unjust judgment are destroying the foundations of life on earth.

Then in verse 6 we read, "I said, 'You are gods....'" This is a reference back to the psalmist's calling the judges "gods" in verse 1: "...He judges in the midst of the gods." The succeeding lines make clear that although the psalmist referred to the wicked judges as "gods," they were not really gods at all and proved themselves not up to the task of being gods. This is made clear in two ways.

First, the second line of verse 6 adds, "And all of you are sons of the Most High." What can this mean? The similar expression "sons of God" is used in the Old Testament only of angels (Gen. 6:2, 4; Job 1:6; 2:1), unless one interprets Genesis 6:1–4 to be speaking of a godly line of men. The Israelite judges were neither angels nor godly men. Hosea 1:10 speaks prophetically of Gentiles becoming "sons of the living God," but this has reference to Gentiles becoming Christians and thus adopted children of God (Rom. 9:26). The judges were not Christians, either. The easiest, if not only, explanation is that they are called "sons of the Most High" in irony. That is, the psalmist calls them "sons of the Most High" not because they really were, but because they thought of themselves as such, and to show up that attitude as ridiculous (see a similar use of irony by Paul in 1 Cor. 4:8). If this is correct, it would imply that they were also called "gods" in irony. Thus the thought would be that these human judges thought of themselves as gods, immortal beings with the power of life and death.

The next lines, in Psalm 82:7, confirm such an interpretation: the judges are told that they are ordinary men who will die. The clear implication is that though they

seemed to rule over the life and death of their fellow Israelites, they were no more gods than anyone else, because—
like even the greatest of men—they will die.

Then, in verse 8, the psalmist addresses God in the second person, "Arise, O God, judge the earth!..." (NASB). In
other words, the judges have proved themselves to be false
gods; now let the true God come and judge the world in
righteousness.

This way of reading Psalm 82 does not conflict with or
undermine Christ's argument in John 10:34–36. When he
says, "If he called them gods, to whom the word of God
came..." (John 10:35 NASB), nothing in the text demands
that the "gods" be anything but false gods. Jesus' argument may be paraphrased and expanded as follows:

> Is it not written in the Law which you call your own, "I said,
> 'You are gods'"? The psalmist, whom you regard as one of
> your own, and yourselves as worthy successors to him,
> called those wicked judges, against whom the word of God
> came in judgment, "gods." And yet the Scripture cannot be
> broken; it must have some fulfillment. Therefore these
> worthless judges must have been called "gods" for a reason,
> to point to some worthy human judge who is rightly called
> God. Now the Father has witnessed to my holy calling and
> sent me into the world to fulfill everything he has purposed.
> That being so, how can you, who claim to follow in the
> tradition of the psalmist, possibly be justified in rejecting the
> fulfillment of his words by accusing me of blasphemy for
> calling myself the Son of God? How can you escape being
> associated with those wicked judges who judged unjustly by
> your unjust judgment of me?

By this interpretation, Jesus is saying that what the Israelite judges were called in irony and condemnation, he is in
reality and in holiness; he *does* what they could not do and
is what they could not be. This kind of positive fulfillment in

Christ contrasted with a human failure in the Old Testament occurs elsewhere in the New Testament, notably the contrast between the sinner Adam and the righteous Christ (Rom. 5:12–21; 1 Cor. 15:21–22, 45).

To summarize, the judges called "gods" in Psalm 82 could not have been really gods, because the Bible denies that mighty or authoritative men are gods. If they are called "gods" in a positive sense, it is strictly a figurative expression for their standing in God's place in judging his people. But more likely they are called "gods" in irony, to expose them as wicked judges who were completely inadequate to the task of exercising divine judgment. However one interprets Psalm 82, then, there is no basis for teaching that there are creatures who may be described qualitatively as gods.

We conclude, then, that the biblical statements that there is only one God are not contradicted or modified one bit by the prooftexts cited by JWs to prove that creatures may be honored as gods. There is one Creator, and all else is created; one Eternal, and all else temporal; one Sovereign Lord, and all else undeserving servants; one God, and all else worshipers. Anything else is a denial of biblical monotheism.

5

▲▼▲▼▲▼▲▼▲▼▲▼▲▼▲▼▲▼▲▼▲▼▲▼▲▼▲

Is Jesus a Creature?

The JWs deny that Jesus is the Creator, arguing in *Should You Believe in the Trinity?* that "the Bible plainly states that in his prehuman existence, Jesus was a created spirit being, just as angels were spirit beings created by God" (p. 14). In support of this claim the booklet cites Proverbs 8:22, Colossians 1:15, and Revelation 3:14. To make the same point, the Arians cited these same texts, especially Proverbs 8:22. We shall consider each of these texts in turn and then point out some of the biblical evidence for regarding Jesus as the Creator rather than a creature.

Is Jesus a Created Wisdom?

In the NWT Proverbs 8:22, in which Wisdom is speaking, begins, "Jehovah himself produced me as the beginning of his way...." The Witnesses claim regarding Wisdom here that "most scholars agree that it is a figure of speech for Jesus as a spirit creature prior to his human existence," and they conclude that the prehuman Jesus was created (p. 14). There are a number of reasons why this interpretation should be rejected.

First, the word that the JWs translate "produced," and that some versions have even rendered "created," is the word *qanah*. This word is used frequently in Proverbs, never with the meaning "create," but always "get" or "buy," that is, get with money (Prov. 1:5; 4:5, 7; 8:22; 15:32; 16:16; 17:16; 18:15; 19:8; 20:14; 23:23). That is also its consistent meaning in the some seventy instances in which it is used elsewhere in the Old Testament.

Second, "wisdom" is personified, not only in Proverbs 8:22–31, but throughout Proverbs 1–9. Nothing in Proverbs 8:22–31 suggests that this is a different "wisdom" than is spoken of in the preceding and following chapters. Therefore, if we take 8:22 to speak literally about Christ, we must also assume that Christ is a woman who cries in the streets (1:20–21), and who lives with someone named "Prudence" (8:12) in a house with seven pillars (9:1)!

Third, the text reads quite naturally as a poetic way of saying that Wisdom preexisted eternally with Jehovah. In previous chapters Solomon has urged his son to "get" *(qanah)* wisdom (Prov. 4:5, 7), and this challenge is continued in later chapters (16:16; 17:16; 19:8). In Proverbs 3:19–20 Solomon states briefly that God exercised wisdom in his work of creation. Throughout Proverbs 1–9, and especially in chapters 8 and 9, wisdom is personified as a woman who calls out to the city to take instruction from her (ch. 8) and to come eat at her table in her house (ch. 9).

In the midst of this highly poetic section of Proverbs appears a passage (8:22–31) that speaks of God's getting *(qanah* again) wisdom before his works, and of his creating the world through wisdom—clearly parallel in meaning to 3:19–20, and just as clearly to be taken as a personification of God's own attribute of wisdom. That is, the point is that after urging his son to "get" wisdom, Solomon answers the child's question, "When did God get wisdom?" by saying, in effect, "God 'got' wisdom in eternity," that is, God has always had wisdom. Thus 8:23 says, "'From everlasting I was established...'" (NASB); the phrase *from everlasting* is the same phrase used of God in Psalm 90:2, where the JWs recognize that God is being described as having no beginning.

As Derek Kidner put it so well in his commentary on Proverbs: "...the present passage makes excellent sense at the level of metaphor: *i.e.* as a powerful way of saying that if *we* must do nothing without wisdom, God Himself has made and done nothing without it. The wisdom by which the world is rightly used is none other than the wisdom by which it exists."[1]

It is unlikely, then, that Proverbs 8:22–31 should be understood as a description of Christ, though some things said of wisdom there may be fulfilled in a deeper sense in Christ, just as 2 Samuel 7:14 was actually speaking about Solomon, though in a prophetic sense it had a greater fulfillment in Christ (Heb. 1:5b). Thus, even assuming that Proverbs 8:22 was a description of Christ, it would be just as much a mistake to argue from Proverbs 8:22 that Christ was created as to argue from 2 Samuel 7:14 that Christ would be a sinner! In fact, it would be a worse mistake, because Proverbs 8:22, carefully interpreted, is not asserting a created origin of wisdom at all, as we have shown. Even if what is said of wisdom in 8:22–31 is applied in some way to Christ, then, it is a poetic affirmation of his having always existed, not a proof that he was created.

"The Firstborn of All Creation"

In Colossians 1:15 Christ is called "the first-born of all creation." This expression is quoted in the Watchtower booklet with no explanatory comment, evidently taking it for granted that it will be understood to mean that Christ is a creature. However, in another Watchtower publication, *Reasoning from the Scriptures,* three arguments are presented for interpreting Colossians 1:15 in this way.

First, the JWs note that the usual trinitarian interpretation takes "firstborn of all creation" to mean that Christ is "the most distinguished in relation to those who were created," and asks why this title is not then applied to the Father and the Holy Spirit.[2] But this is simply an argument from silence—that is, it reasons that because something isn't said, it isn't so. Such arguments are notoriously unreliable. For example, because Matthew 28:1 mentions only two women who visited the tomb of Jesus, should we conclude that *only* two women went? No, because Luke 24:10 makes it clear that at least five women visited the tomb. The Bible never says explicitly (not even in the NWT) that God the Father is Jehovah. But of course he is Jehovah, because it does say that the Father is the only true God (John 17:3), and from the Old Testament we know that Jehovah is the only true God (e.g., Jer. 10:10).

Moreover, there is a good reason why "firstborn of all creation" is never applied to the Father or the Holy Spirit. The JWs are on to something when they claim that the idea of sonship cannot be eliminated from the word *firstborn.* But they have not represented trinitarians' understanding of that word fairly. Trinitarians believe that the word does not merely mean something as vague as "most distinguished," but rather that it means the *heir,* the one who stands to inherit his father's estate. Christ, as the Son of God, is the Father's "heir" because everything that is the Father's is also the Son's. Of course, this is a figure of speech, and should not be pressed too literally (God the

Father will never die and "leave his inheritance" to the Son!). The point is simply that just as we say a man's firstborn son is usually the heir of all his property, so Colossians 1:15 calls Christ the "firstborn [heir] of all creation."

Second, the Witnesses point out that the parallel expressions "firstborn of Pharaoh," "firstborn of Israel," and so on, are always used to mean the first one born in that group, so that "firstborn of all creation" must mean the first one created. To be more exact, however, what these expressions mean is the first child of the one named—thus, the firstborn of Pharaoh is Pharaoh's first son; the firstborn of Israel is Israel's first son; and so on. If the expression "firstborn of all creation" is held to be parallel to these phrases, it would then mean the first son (or offspring) of all creation. However, this would be the exact opposite of what the text actually says, which is that all creation came into existence through Christ (Col. 1:16). Creation did not produce Christ; Christ produced creation! Therefore, since the meaning "first child of" will not fit the context, the meaning of "heir" must be understood. Only this interpretation makes sense of the text, which then means that Christ is the heir of creation because all things were made through him and for him.

An illustration may help clarify what is at issue here. If we read the phrase "the heir of John Smith," we would have no trouble understanding that the one called an heir was also (probably) a child of John Smith. However, if the same person were called "the heir of the Smith estate," we would realize immediately that the one called an heir was neither part of the estate nor a child of the estate! Nor would we be confused if we read "the heir of the Smith family"; although this expression would be unusual, we would understand that the heir is a member of the Smith family. The point of this parallel should be obvious. "All creation" cannot be understood as the parent of Jesus Christ. Nor can it be understood as the "family" of which he is a part, not even in the JWs' view, since then God would have to be included in that "family" called "all creation." This leaves only the possibility that "all creation" is the estate that Christ "inherits" by virtue of being God's Son, the one for whom all creation was made (v. 16).

Finally, the JWs render the phrase "all things" in Colossians 1:16–20 as "all [other] things" four times in order to imply that Christ is one of the created things. They justify this insertion by appealing to such texts as Luke 13:2, where "other" is clearly implied. This argument overlooks two key facts. First, the term for "all" in Colossians 1:16–20 is not merely the general word for "all," *pas,* but *ta panta,* a neuter plural form used to mean "the entirety" or "the whole," and which, when used of creation, means "the universe," all created things without exception (*see, for example,* Eph. 1:10–11 NWT). Second, the insertion also changes the meaning of the text, rather than making explicit what is already obvious, as in Luke 13:2. That is, the word *other* can be omitted from a text like Luke 13:2 without changing the obvious meaning; but Colossians 1:16–20 reads very differently depending on whether or not the word *other* is added.

In conclusion, Colossians 1:15 certainly cannot be used to *prove* that Christ is created. The interpretation "heir of all creation" fits the context and understands "firstborn" in a legitimate figurative sense. The JWs' reading of the text requires them to add "other" four times to the following verses to force the text to agree with their view, and it still does not really make good sense of the expression "firstborn of all creation." Thus, if anything, this passage is a powerful prooftext for Christ as the Creator.[3]

The Beginning of God's Creation

Revelation 3:14 calls Christ "the Amen, the faithful and true witness, and the beginning of the creation of God." The use of the word *beginning* as a description of Christ is said by JWs to indicate that he was created. If one considers the range of possible meanings of the Greek word *archē* translated "beginning," it must be admitted that the word might bear this meaning. However, that is not the only or even a likely meaning.

The main argument presented by the JW booklet for taking "beginning of the creation" in the sense of "first creation" is that John (the author of the Book of Revelation) always uses *archē* "with the common meaning of 'beginning'" (p. 14). However, if by "beginning" one understands "first thing," this is not so. In fact, it has this meaning only once in John's writings (John 2:11). Elsewhere in John's Gospel and Epistles it always refers to a beginning point *in time* (John 1:1, 2; 6:64; 8:25, 44; 15:27; 16:4; 1 John 1:1; 2:7, 13, 14, 24; 3:8, 11; 2 John 5, 6), not the first thing in a series. In the Book of Revelation, in fact, *archē* is used only three other times, and always of God as "the beginning and the end" (Rev. 1:8; 21:6; 22:13). Yet Witnesses will rightly deny that God is a first thing in a series of other things.

Thus it is at least possible, if not probable, that Revelation 3:14 does not use "beginning" in the sense of "first thing." We must therefore consider two alternate interpretations, both of which are consistent with the Trinity.

First, it might be that in Revelation 3:14 *archē* means "ruler" or "first over" creation. The argument for this view is a simple one. It would appear that wherever else in the New Testament the word *archē* is used of a person, it nearly always refers to a ruler of some sort. (The only exceptions are the three uses in Revelation of the expression "the beginning and the end" for God.) In particular, the plural form *archai* frequently occurs in the New Testament and is usually translated "principalities" or the like (Luke 12:11; Rom. 8:38; Eph. 3:10; 6:12; Col. 1:16; 2:15; Titus 3:1). Twice it is used in the singular to mean "rule" or "domain" (Luke 20:20; Jude 6). Three times it occurs in the expression "all rule" or "every ruler" (1 Cor. 15:24; Eph. 1:21; Col. 2:10).

Moreover, in Colossians 1:18, the only other place in the New Testament where Christ is called *archē*, where it is usually translated "beginning," the meaning "ruler" is practically certain. This is because the plural *archai* occurs three times in that context (1:16; 2:10, 15) with the meaning "rulers," and since Colossians 1:18 ("the *archē*, the first-born from the dead") is clearly parallel to Revelation 1:5 ("the firstborn from the dead, and the *archōn* [ruler] of the kings of the earth").

This line of reasoning has much merit, and it is possible that "ruler" is the correct meaning of *archē* in Revelation 3:14. However, it is not certain, as it is also possible that *archē* means "source" or "first cause."

The Greek word *archē* could, in first-century Greek, bear the meaning of "first cause" or "origin" or "source," when used in relation to the universe or creation. Although this usage does not appear to be clearly found elsewhere in the New Testament, in the Book of Revelation *archē* appears to be used with this meaning in all three of the other occurrences of the word in that book. In these three verses, God is called "the beginning and the end" (1:8; 21:6; 22:13). The best interpretation of this expression would seem to be that God is the beginner and the consummator of creation—that he is its first cause and its final goal. It is therefore reasonable to think that the same usage is found in 3:14.

In response to this line of reasoning, it may be replied that the fact that Jesus is not here called "the end" as well as "the beginning" suggests that the word is being used with a different nuance. This observation does not disprove the "first cause" interpretation, but it does indicate that such is not the only possible interpretation.

In short, *archē* in Revelation 3:14 could mean either "ruler" or "first cause." The meaning of "first thing created" is the least likely interpretation, if context and the use of *archē* in the New Testament with reference to persons are taken into consideration. Certainly Revelation 3:14 cannot be used to *prove* that Christ is created.

Jesus as Creator

So far we have looked at the three main prooftexts used by JWs (and many other antitrinitarians) to prove that Christ is a creature. We have seen that certainly none of these texts says so clearly, and all three are better interpreted as teaching that Christ is the eternal Creator. Therefore, if the Bible elsewhere gives clear testimony to Christ as the Creator, we may safely conclude that these prooftexts agree with that teaching.

That the Bible does clearly teach that Christ created all things is fairly easy to show. "All things came into existence through him, and apart from him not even one thing came into existence" (John 1:3 NWT). If *all things* that "came into existence" did so through Christ, then he cannot have "come into existence" himself. We have already mentioned Colossians 1:16, which states that "all things were created in him, in the heavens and upon the earth, the visible and the invisible, whether thrones or lordships or governments or authorities; all things have been created through him and for him" (translating literally; compare the *Kingdom Interlinear Translation* [KIT], published by the Watchtower Society). If all the things that were created were created in, through, and for him, it follows that he himself was not created. Hebrews 1:2 says, "through whom [the Son] he [God] made the ages" (KIT). This implies, of course, that the Son transcends the ages.

The JWs try to turn this evidence on its head by pointing out that these texts all say that God made the world *through* Christ, and conclude from this that Christ was God's "junior partner, as it were" (p. 7), in the work of creation. They note that in 1 Corinthians 8:6 creation is said to have come *from* the Father, but *through* Jesus.

There are at least two reasons why this objection cannot be valid. First, the New Testament also states that the world came *through* God (Rom. 11:36), specifically through the Father (Heb. 2:10). (The same Greek word translated "through" *[dia]* or its contracted form *[di']* appears in all these verses.) This means that "through" does not imply a lesser or secondary role in creation, as the JWs claim. This is apparently so embarrassing to the Witnesses that they translated *di'* as "by" instead of "through" in Romans 11:36—"Because from him and by *[di']* him and for *[eis]* him are all things" (NWT). It is also noteworthy that Romans 11:36 says that all things are "for" *(eis)* God, whereas Colossians 1:16 says that all things are "for" *(eis)* Christ.

Second, the Bible teaches that God made the world all by himself. "I, Jehovah, am doing everything, stretching out the heavens by myself, laying out the earth. Who was with me?" (Isa. 44:24 NWT). Of course, the rhetorical question "Who was with me?" invites the answer "No one." Therefore, it is simply impossible from a biblical standpoint to hold that God created Christ and then created everything

else through him. The idea that the supreme God required a
''junior partner'' to do the dirty work of creating the world is
a pagan idea, not a biblical one, as we saw in our discussion
of the history of trinitarian theology in chapter 4.

6

Does the Bible Deny
That Jesus Is God?

Thus far in our examination of the biblical teaching relevant to the Trinity we have seen that there is only one true God, all other so-called gods being false gods; and that Jesus is the Creator, not a creature.

The JWs will claim, however, that other lines of evidence from Scripture rule out the possibility that Jesus is God. We will consider some of these arguments in this chapter.

Jesus Distinguished from God

The most basic sort of argument employed by JWs to show that Jesus cannot be God is this: There are several Scriptures that distinguish between Jesus and God, treating them as different individuals. Some of these Scriptures simply distinguish between Jesus and the Father (e.g., John 8:17–18). These texts present no difficulty for the trinitarian position, since the Trinity doctrine also distinguishes between the Father and the Son as two "persons."

Then there are texts that speak of the Father as the God of Jesus Christ (e.g., John 20:17; 1 Cor. 11:3). The

Watchtower booklet argues, "Since Jesus *had* a God, his Father, he could not at the same time *be* that God" (p. 17). But again, trinitarians do not hold that Jesus is his Father. They hold that Jesus, because he became a man, was placed in a position in which as man he was required to honor the Father as his God. At the same time, trinitarians may point out some aspects of the Bible's teaching that show that JWs have misunderstood the implications of the Father being Christ's God.

First, Jesus made it clear that the Father was his God in a unique manner compared with the manner in which the Father is our God. Thus, in John 20:17 Jesus stated, "I am ascending to my Father and YOUR Father and to my God and YOUR God" (NWT). Why did Jesus not simply say, "I am ascending to our Father and our God"? In fact, Jesus never spoke of the Father as "our Father," including himself along with his disciples. (In Matt. 6:9 Jesus told the disciples that *they* should pray, "Our Father...," but did not include himself in that prayer.) Jesus was careful to distinguish the two relationships, because he was God's Son *by nature*, whereas Christians are God's "sons" *by adoption*. Similarly, the Father was Jesus' God because Jesus humbled himself to become a man (Phil. 2:7), whereas the Father is our God because we are by nature creatures.

Second, in the immediate context of John 20:17 it is made clear that whatever relation Jesus has with the Father, the relationship that we disciples have with Jesus is that he is our "Lord" and our "God" (John 20:28). (We will have more to say about John 20:28 in chapter 7.)

Then there are texts that simply refer to "God" alongside Christ in such a way as to distinguish them. For instance, 1 Timothy 5:21 speaks of "God and Christ Jesus," and 1 Corinthians 8:6 distinguishes between "one God, the Father," and "one Lord, Jesus Christ." But trinitarians have a simple answer: These texts refer to the Father as "God" not because Jesus Christ is less than God, but simply because the title *God* was normally used of the Father.

An analogy may help, if it is not pressed beyond the point it seeks to illustrate. If someone says, "Bush appeared with Barbara," they do not mean to imply that only George has the name Bush, or that Barbara's last name is not Bush; their usage is simply determined by the fact that George is the one usually called Bush. Now, this analogy has a problem, in that George and Barbara are two separate Bushes, whereas the Father and the Son are not two Gods. But this difference is *precisely what we would expect* when comparing the infinite God with finite humans.

That these texts cannot mean that Jesus is not God can be proved from some of the very texts themselves. As we have said, 1 Corinthians 8:6 distinguishes between "one God, the Father," and "one Lord, Jesus Christ." The JWs conclude from this verse that since the Father is the "one God," Jesus cannot be God. But by that reasoning, since Jesus is the "one Lord," the Father cannot be Lord! Yet we know that the Father *is* Lord (Matt. 11:25). Therefore, there must be something wrong with this reasoning. What is wrong with it, as has been explained, is that it assumes that the use of a title for one person rules out its application to another. This cannot be assumed, but must be determined by considering all of the relevant biblical teaching.

Finally, 1 Timothy 2:5 says that Jesus is the "one mediator between God and men" (NWT), and from this statement the JW booklet concludes that Jesus cannot be God, because "by definition a mediator is someone separate from those who need mediation" (p. 16). But by this reasoning Jesus cannot be a man, either; yet this very text says that he is "a man"! The truth is that Jesus is able to mediate between God and men because he is himself both God and man.

The Paradoxes of Jesus

Several understandably popular arguments against the belief that Jesus is God are based on various paradoxes that arise when one compares what the Bible says about Jesus with what it says about God. The JW booklet discusses some of these. God cannot be tempted, yet Jesus was tempted (pp. 14–15); God is greater than angels, yet Jesus was lower than them (p. 15); God cannot be seen, yet Jesus was seen (p. 16); God cannot die, yet Jesus did die (p. 18); God knows everything, yet Jesus had limited knowledge and learned (p. 19). To these, other such paradoxes can be added. God is eternal, yet Jesus was born; God never changes, yet Jesus grew; God does not get tired, yet Jesus got tired. All these paradoxes rest on one basic paradox: God is not a man, yet Jesus was a man.

One would think that in a booklet on the Trinity that raises these paradoxes the trinitarian answer to them would at least be mentioned. But such is not the case. Trinitarians believe that Jesus was both God *and* man. To be more precise, they believe that Jesus was a single divine person (the second person of the Trinity) in whom were united two natures—his own divine nature, which he has always had, and human nature, which he took upon himself in order to redeem mankind.

The usual response to this doctrine by JWs is puzzlement. How can Jesus be both God and man? Isn't that contradictory and unreasonable?

Trinitarians believe that it is not unreasonable or self-contradictory to say that Jesus was and is both God and man. It would be contradictory if we were asserting that Jesus' flesh was itself divine, or that his divine nature was mortal. But such assertions do not represent classic trinitarianism. What we do assert is that God, without ceasing to be God, took to himself human nature, not by mixing the two together, but by uniting them in the one person of Jesus. This is difficult to comprehend or understand fully, just as is the doctrine of the Trinity itself, but it is not self-contradictory.[1]

For example, Jesus was tempted. But trinitarians do not believe that his temptation derived in any sense from his divine nature, but rather was a result of his living as a human being in a corrupt world where temptations abound. Thus God, *as God,* cannot be tempted; but Jesus, who is both God and man, *as man* and living in a fallen earth, was tempted.

Moreover, the JW booklet overlooks certain relevant teachings about Jesus that put these paradoxes in a different light. Yes, God is not a man (Num. 23:19), while Jesus is (1 Tim. 2:5); yet Jesus is also God (John 20:28). Yes, God cannot be tempted (James 1:13), while Jesus was tempted (Heb. 4:15); yet Jesus could not sin (John 5:19). Yes, God knows all things (Isa. 41:22–23), while Jesus did not know the day of his return (Mark 13:32); yet Jesus did know all things (John 16:30). Yes, God cannot be seen (John 1:18), while men did see Jesus (1 John 1:1–2); yet no man has seen or can see Jesus (1 Tim. 6:16). Yes, God cannot die (1 Tim. 1:17), while Jesus did die (Phil. 2:8); yet no one could take Jesus' life from him (John 10:18), it was impossible for him to remain dead (Acts 2:24), and he raised himself (John 2:19–22). Yes, God never changes (Ps. 102:26–27), while Jesus grew (Luke 2:52) and learned (Heb. 5:8); yet Jesus also never changes (Heb. 1:10–12; 13:8). Yes, God is eternal (Ps. 90:2), while Jesus was born (Matt. 1:18); yet Jesus has always existed (John 8:58).

These biblical facts rule out the possibility of resolving the paradox by simply denying that Jesus was God. Nor is it possible to resolve the paradox by denying his humanity, as some Gnostics did. Nor is it legitimate to resolve it by saying that Jesus was a mere man in whom God dwelled, as God might also be said to dwell in other men, even if to a lesser extent. These theories were all put forward in the early centuries of the church and were all rejected by the orthodox, and for good reason: they simply don't fit with what the Bible says about Jesus. They are less mysterious, less paradoxical, but they flatly contradict the Bible.

It must be kept in mind that none of these passages that talk about Jesus being born, growing, learning, withstanding temptation, getting tired, dying, and so forth, draws the conclusion that JWs do from these facts. That is, the Bible never comes out and says, "Therefore, Jesus is not God," or anything of the sort. What we have are statements about Jesus that the Witnesses *think* are incompatible with his being God. But this is a matter of inference, not a matter of explicit statement. Moreover, these statements are not, strictly speaking, contradictory to the idea that Jesus was God, as has been explained.

The Ransom Sacrifice of Jesus

The Witnesses believe that if Jesus had been God, his death would not have been a fitting sacrifice because it would have exceeded God's just requirement. The JW booklet explains:

> Jesus, no more and no less than a perfect human, became a ransom that compensated exactly for what Adam lost—the right to perfect human life on earth.... The perfect human life of Jesus was the "corresponding ransom" [1 Tim. 2:6 NWT] required by divine justice—no more, no less.... If Jesus, however, were part of a Godhead, the ransom price would have been infinitely higher than what God's own Law required [p. 15].

It should be noted that once again the JWs have constructed an argument based on what they suppose is a valid inference from their understanding of the significance of Christ's death. The Bible never draws the conclusion that Jesus could not have been anything more than a mere man.

Moreover, this argument betrays the Witnesses' real view of Jesus. While they admit that Jesus had a "prehuman existence," this does not mean that the man Jesus was that same powerful spirit creature who JWs think was God's "junior partner" in creating the world. Rather, the Witness view is that at the moment of Jesus' conception in the womb of Mary, the prehuman spirit called "the Word" (John 1:1) or God's "Son" (Heb. 1:2) *ceased to exist,* and a human person was *created* by Jehovah with the memories of the former spirit creature. Thus, according to the Witnesses, Jesus on earth was *not* the "Mighty God" (Isa. 9:6), but only a mere man with the memories of that Mighty God.

This leads to a curious conclusion: JWs can give no reason why God needed to send his Son to earth as a man at all. Since all that was required was a perfect human, God could simply have created one "from scratch," if he had wanted.

The JWs' argument concerning the "corresponding ransom" also suffers from at least two more direct problems. The first is that translating "corresponding ransom" for *antilutron* in 1 Timothy 2:6, if "corresponding" is taken to mean "no more, no less," is a clear case of overtranslation—of reading more into the word than is really there. Although the word is very rare in Greek, and it appears only here in the Bible, the meaning is certainly the same as Christ's statement in Mark 10:45 that he came to give his life as "a ransom in exchange for *[lutron anti]* many" (NWT). The idea in both passages is simply that of substitution—of Christ's taking our place. The idea that this required that Christ be "no more" than a perfect human is absent.

Second, the JWs' claim that Christ's death was meant to be merely the sacrifice of one perfect human to make up for the sin of one human, Adam, is contradicted by Mark 10:45, which says that Christ was "a ransom in exchange for *many*." Thus, Christ was not merely one man dying for one other man; he was dying for millions of men, women, and children. Christ is called the "last Adam" and contrasted with Adam (Rom. 5:12–21; 1 Cor. 15:21–22, 45), but this does not prove that he was "no more" than Adam.

The Submission of Jesus to God

Perhaps the most frequently heard argument against Jesus being God by nature and equal in deity to the Father is the biblical teaching regarding Jesus' submission to the Father. The JWs realize that trinitarians believe that in his human nature Christ was in a position of submission to the Father. However, the Witnesses argue that this cannot account for Jesus submitting to God after his resurrection from the dead and ascension to heaven.

Thus, JWs, although they do quote Scriptures that speak of Christ's humble position relative to the Father while a man on earth (especially John 14:28), rely even more so on Scriptures that speak of Christ's submission after his resurrection. For instance, they note that 1 Corinthians 11:3 says that "God is the head of Christ"; 1 Corinthians 15:28 says that the Son will subject himself to God the Father after sin and death have been eliminated; and various Scriptures say that even now, after Christ's ascension, the Father is Christ's God (e.g., John 20:17; Rom. 15:6; 1 Cor. 15:24; 2 Cor. 1:3; Rev. 1:6; 3:12). On the basis of these Scriptures, they conclude that Jesus was not simply lower than the Father temporarily while on earth, but will always be in submission to God.

Two points may be made that will show that none of these Scriptures contradicts the Bible's teaching that Jesus Christ is God. First, the JWs' argument assumes that Jesus is no longer a man. The Witnesses believe that the physical body of Jesus was never raised to life, but was "raised" ("recreated" might be more accurate) as a mere spirit. If Jesus' body was raised from the dead, though, as trinitarians believe, then as a man Jesus would still naturally be in some sense required to submit to the Father as his God.

Although this is not the place for an extended discussion of the nature of Christ's resurrection, a few short remarks are in order. The Bible explicitly states that Jesus Christ, since his resurrection and ascension, is "a man"; he is the mediator of the new covenant as a man (1 Tim. 2:5), and he will judge the world as a man (Acts 17:31). Jesus also flatly denied being a mere spirit (Luke 24:39). Before his death, Jesus had prophesied that he would raise his own body from the dead (John 2:19–22), which of course also implies that Jesus was God. Jesus also said that he would surrender his "soul," or physical life, in order to receive it again (John 10:17–18). Peter preached on Pentecost that Jesus could not be kept dead and that his *flesh* lived in hope of the resurrection of his *soul* from Hades (Acts 2:24–32), which of course implies that Jesus' flesh was raised from the dead.

The JWs argue that Jesus could not be raised with his physical body because that would have involved taking back the "ransom price" he paid for our salvation. As we have seen, the Witnesses have some misunderstandings about Christ's "ransom." Once again, this argument is based on an inference that the Bible does not support. Jesus gave his *soul* as a ransom (Mark 10:45), and he had the right to receive his soul back again (John 10:17–18), based on God's promise that his soul would not remain in Hades (Acts 2:27).

The JWs also point to the passages in the Gospels where the disciples did not recognize Jesus at first. But in each case the text gives a different explanation than that he was a mere spirit: the disciples' eyes were kept from recognizing him (Luke 24:16, 31); Mary Magdalene was crying in the early dawn and not even facing Jesus at first (John 20:11-16); the disciples in the boat were far from shore, and it was again barely dawn (John 21:4-7).

There are a few other biblical passages quoted by JWs to prove that Christ's physical body was not raised, but these have also been misinterpreted.[2] The point, once again, is that if Jesus was raised as a human being—albeit a glorified, exalted, immortal human being—he would continue to submit to the Father as his God by virtue of his being a man.

The second point that ought to be made about the submission of the Son to the Father after his resurrection and ascension is that such submission is in no way inconsistent with the Trinity. The doctrine of the Trinity maintains that the three persons are equal to one another in essence or nature, and it leaves open the question of how the three persons relate to one another within the Trinity. Thus, while trinitarians insist that Christ is just as much God as the Father, they do not deny that the Son is in some sense submissive to the Father even after his ascension.

An examination of the "subordinationist" texts cited by JWs bears out this point. For example, 1 Corinthians 11:3 says that "God is the head of Christ." But it also says that Christ is the head of every man, and that the man (that is, the husband) is the head of the woman (that is, his wife). Now, the Bible is very clear that men and women are equal in terms of nature; both are fully human, both are in God's image, and in Christ they are one (Gen. 1:26-28; Gal. 3:28). Female submission, then, is a matter of function or position or role, not of essential superiority of the man over the woman. As for Christ's being the head of every man, in context this also refers to a functional headship, not an essential superiority. And in one sense Christ is not essentially superior to men, since Christ himself is a man, as we have seen. Of course, in another sense Christ is far superior to men in essence, since Christ is also God.

The fact that Christ's submission to the Father is so often assumed to prove inferiority of nature actually reveals something about our mistaken, and sinful, attitude toward authority and submission. We assume that whoever is "on top" must be there because he is somehow "better." We regard submission as an undesirable position. But the persons of the Trinity evidently do not feel that way. Each of the three persons delights in glorifying the others. Thus the Son wants to be glorified by the Father only so that he may thus bring more glory to the Father (John 17:1). The Holy Spirit comes solely for the purpose of glorifying the Son (John 16:14). The Father exalts Jesus before the world and calls on all to honor him as Lord, that is, as Jehovah; yet, this brings glory to God the Father (Phil. 2:9–11). There is no competition among the persons of the Trinity for glory, honor, or power; if anything, the persons of the Trinity are zealously working to bring glory to one another.

Jesus as the "Only-Begotten Son"

The JWs claim that the description of Christ as the "only-begotten Son" indicates that the Son was created. They argue that the term "only-begotten" (in Greek, *monogenēs*) does include the idea of begetting, and therefore that Jesus was begotten by the Father. Noting that trinitarians claim the word as applied to Jesus means "a sort of only son relationship without the begetting" (which is how only a minority of trinitarians would define the word), the Witness booklet asks, "Does that sound logical to you? Can a man father a son without begetting him?" (p. 15).

Pointing out that Isaac is called Abraham's "only-begotten son" in Hebrews 11:17, the booklet continues, "There can be no question that in Isaac's case, he was only-begotten in the normal sense" (p. 16). Actually, this claim is open to serious question. Isaac was *not* Abraham's only-begotten son in the literal sense of the *only* son Abraham begat. Abraham had many other sons, including Ishmael, who was begotten by Abraham before Isaac. Thus, Isaac is called Abraham's "only-begotten son" in the sense of Abraham's *unique* or special son.

After quoting from some scholarly works in apparent agreement with JWs' interpretation of "only-begotten," the booklet concludes that "Almighty God can rightly be called his [Jesus'] Begetter, or Father, in the same sense that an earthly father, like Abraham, begets a son" (p. 16).

If this line of reasoning were sound, however, it would suggest a conclusion rather embarrassing to JWs. For if God is Jesus' Father "in the same sense that an earthly father... begets a son," then it would seem that Jesus must have had a heavenly Mother, as well as a heavenly Father. Of course, JWs would cringe at such a suggestion. Unlike Mormons, for example, the Witnesses deny that the pre-human Jesus was begotten through a divine Mother. Yet their argument seems to point to such a conclusion.

We may make this point in another way. The JWs are employing an argument having the following logical form: (a) All sons are begotten; (b) the prehuman Jesus was a son; therefore (c) Jesus was begotten; but (d) all who are begotten also begin to exist at some point in time, and are thus creatures; therefore (e) Jesus, having been begotten, must also be a creature. This sounds good, and it is logically valid, meaning that *if* the premises, or assertions of fact on which the argument is based, are true, then the conclusion would also have to be true. But consider the following parallel argument: (a) All sons had mothers; (b) the prehuman Jesus was a son; therefore (c) the prehuman Jesus had a mother. The argument may also be put this way: (d) All who are begotten have a mother; therefore (e) Jesus, having been begotten, also had a mother.

There are only two ways to escape this argument. The first is to point out that the Bible does not *say* that Jesus had a heavenly Mother. This does not actually refute the argument, but it shows that biblically there may be something wrong with it. The second is to argue that what is true of earthly fathers and sons need not be true of the divine Father and his divine Son. What this does is to show that the statements "all sons had mothers" and "all who are begotten had mothers" are hasty generalizations—they are only true of *earthly* beings.

These same responses, however, may also be made to the JWs' arguments to prove that Jesus must have had a beginning. The Bible does not actually *say* that the prehuman Jesus was begotten by the Father *at some point in time;* it does not say that he had a beginning. (We have already noted that Prov. 8:22, Col. 1:15, and Rev. 3:14 do not support such a conclusion.) Moreover, what is true of earthly fathers and sons (that the sons are always younger than the fathers and are born in time) is not necessarily true of the eternal Father and his Son.

The Watchtower booklet argues, "Trinitarians say that since God is eternal, so the Son of God is eternal. But how can a person be a son and at the same time be as old as his father?" (p. 15). The answer is, he can't, *if he is a literal son.* And as we have seen, Jesus cannot be considered a literal son of God. But the JW booklet, oblivious to this problem, claims that when the Bible called Jesus God's Son, "it meant 'Son' in a literal way, as with a natural father and son, not as some mysterious part of a Trinity Godhead" (p. 29).

The better question to ask is how an eternal, infinite, divine Father could possibly have a temporal, finite, creaturely son. If *Son* as applied to the prehuman Jesus is at all a description of his nature, and not (as when applied to angels or men) a completely symbolic expression picturing our relationship to God, then we would expect the Son to be the same kind of being as his Father in every substantial respect. This is, in fact, what the Bible says about the Son.

Can Jesus Be God's Son and Also Be God?

The Witnesses' reasoning on this question seems so logical. How can Jesus be "God's Son" and also be God? How can someone be his own son? Isn't that unreasonable and illogical?

Yes, it is unreasonable to say that someone is his own son, but that is not what trinitarianism teaches. The doctrine of the Trinity does not understand Jesus to be his own father, or understand God the Father to be his own son. As has been necessary to repeat many times in this book, the Father and the Son are two distinct persons in the Trinity.

True, Jesus is called the Son *of God,* and not simply the Son of the Father (though he is called that as well [2 John 3]). But this is to be understood as using the title *God* with reference specifically to the Father, without denying that it also applies with equal validity to the Son. To use a useful but limited analogy, if someone referred to me as "Robert Bowman's son," they would be right, even though "Robert Bowman" is my name, because it is also my father's name. (Recall the analogy of George and Barbara Bush sharing the same last name, and the limitations of that analogy.) In other words, "Son of God" is short for "Son of God the Father."

The designation of Jesus as the "Son of God," far from being a disproof of Jesus' essential equality with God, is one of the most important proofs of that truth found in the Bible. (Here it is important to keep in mind that the Trinity doctrine holds the Son to be equal to the Father in *essence* or nature, and it does not deny that the Son obeys the Father or seeks his honor.) The following considerations will show this to be the case.

1. There are numerous examples in Scripture of the word *son* being used figuratively to mean nothing other than "possessing the nature of"; for example, "the sons of disobedience" in Ephesians 2:1 means those who are disobedient. The expression "Son of man" means not that Jesus was literally a son of a man (he had no human father!) but that he was himself a man.

2. There is no doubting that Jesus is called the Son of God in a nonliteral sense, since he was not physically procreated. This point has already been made at some length.

3. It is also certain that Jesus is called the Son of God in a unique sense, since he is called the *monogenēs* Son of God. For the point being made here, it does not matter whether *monogenēs* is understood to mean "only-begotten" or "unique," since even "only-begotten" implies that there is something unique about the sense in which Jesus is God's Son.

4. The Son of God, according to the New Testament, does possess the nature of God fully and completely (Col. 2:9; Heb. 1:2). Therefore, it is reasonable to take the title *Son* as meaning that he possesses his Father's nature.

5. A physical son shares his father's nature, including the fact that both the father and the son had a beginning (though the father's beginning was earlier). Since the Son of

God shares his Father's nature, it is logical that he should share his Father's lack of a beginning.

6. That Jesus did not have a beginning is confirmed by several Scriptures (John 1:1; 8:58; 17:5; Col. 1:17; Heb. 1:2).

7. That this reasoning is valid is confirmed by the fact that Jesus' detractors among the Jews understood his claims to be the unique Son of God in basically this sense. In both John 5:17–18 and John 10:30–39 the Jewish leaders sought to kill Jesus for blasphemy, because they understood his claim to be the Son of God to be the same as claiming equality with God. This understanding persisted despite the fact that Jesus was, as JWs will certainly agree, a masterful communicator. When they handed him over to Pilate, they gave the same reason: Jesus' claim to be God's Son violated their law (against blasphemy) and was deserving of death.

On this last point, it is not sufficient to claim that the Jews simply misunderstood Jesus, as the JW booklet argues (pp. 24–25). One must first show that the preceding independent reasons for understanding "Son of God" as a claim to equality with God are in error. Then one must also explain why it is that Jesus never simply denied being God.

For instance, his saying that "the Son can do nothing of himself" (John 5:19a) was not a denial of being essentially equal with God, but in fact was a tacit claim to equality: Jesus, as the Son, *could not* do anything but what God does! If Jesus was a mere man, and nothing more, he certainly could have done something contrary to what God would do. If the Jews misunderstood Jesus at all, it was in thinking that his claim to do works that only God could do was a claim to be equal with God as an independent, second God—a misunderstanding that Jesus rebuts by saying that he does nothing on his own. Jesus then goes on to assert that he does whatever the Father does (vv. 19b–20), will raise from the dead whomever he wishes, a prerogative belonging to God (v. 21), and will be the final judge of all mankind (v. 22). As a consequence, Jesus says, everyone should give the same honor to the Son—that is, to him, Jesus—that is due to the Father (v. 23). That is hardly a convincing way to deny claiming equality with God!

The same pattern emerges in John 10. The Jews' very complaint was that by calling God his own Father (and thereby regarding himself as God's unique Son), Jesus was making himself out to be God (John 10:30–33). The Watchtower booklet states that in Jesus' response he "forcefully argued that his words were not a claim to be God" (p. 24). This is interesting, because on this basis the NWT rendering of the Jews' charge against Jesus, "you, although being a man, make yourself *a god*," must be considered incorrect. But Jesus in John 10:34–36 certainly did not deny that he was God. He simply reasserted more emphatically what had scandalized the Jews to begin with, namely, that he was the unique Son of God. Again, if there was any misunderstanding that Jesus wished to rebut, it was that his claim to equality with God involved a claim to be an independent God. Jesus then went on to say that the proof of his claim was to be found in the fact that he did works that only God could do (John 10:37–38). The result was that the Jews "tried again to seize him" (10:39 NWT), obviously because they still understood him to be claiming to be God. It is noteworthy that in the booklet the JWs stop at verse 36 and fail to consider the significance of verses 37–39.

Seen in this light, John 10:30 should be understood as a claim by Jesus to essential oneness with God. The JW booklet, noting that elsewhere the same neuter word for "one" *(hen)* implies only unity of purpose (John 17:21–22; 1 Cor. 3:6, 8), concludes that such functional unity is all that is meant in John 10:30. The booklet also quotes John

Calvin, who, though a trinitarian, interpreted the verse along similar lines (p. 24). But while *hen* need not, of itself, mean more than functional unity, in the context of John 10 it surely means much more.

We conclude, then, that nothing in the Bible denies that Jesus is God. Indeed, the Bible teaches that he is the One who created all things, that he is eternal, that he possesses the very nature of God, and that he is essentially equal to God. And all these truths have been seen primarily from biblical passages that JWs think support *their* view of Christ as a creature! We turn next to even more positive evidence from the Bible that Jesus is God.

7

▲▼▲▼▲▼▲▼▲▼▲▼▲▼▲▼▲▼▲▼▲▼▲▼▲▼▲▼▲

Jesus Christ Is God

Modern Scholarship and Jesus as God

Before examining the biblical evidence for the belief that Jesus is God, it may be helpful to respond to the JWs' use of an unidentified article from the *Bulletin of the John Rylands Library* which they quote to prove that biblical scholars agree with them that Jesus was not God.

First, the JW booklet *Should You Believe in the Trinity?* quotes this article as stating: "The fact has to be faced that New Testament research over, say, the last thirty or forty years has been leading an increasing number of biblical scholars to the conclusion that Jesus... certainly never believed himself to be God" (p. 20). This is a correct assessment of modern biblical scholarship, but the Witness booklet has omitted a part of the sentence that puts this fact in an altogether different light. The full sentence reads (with the omitted portion emphasized):

> Yet be that as it may, the fact has to be faced that New Testament research over, say, the last thirty or forty years has been leading an increasing number of biblical scholars

to the conclusion that Jesus *himself may not have claimed any of the christological titles which the Gospels ascribe to him, not even the functional designation "Christ,"* and certainly never believed himself to be God.[1]

That is, the same biblical scholars who deny that Jesus claimed to be God also doubt that he called himself the "Christ," or Messiah. The JWs can hardly claim this judgment to be a reliable one.

Next, the JW booklet quotes the same article when it says, concerning the early Christians, "When, therefore, they assigned him such honorific titles as Christ, Son of man, Son of God and Lord, these were ways of saying not that he was God, but that he did God's work" (p. 20). Note that the article states that the early Christians "assigned" these titles to Jesus. The point here is that Jesus, in these scholars' opinion, did not claim to be Christ, Son of man, Son of God, or Lord! Moreover, they are not claiming that Jesus *or* the early Christians regarded Jesus as a pre-existent divine creature under God who became a man. Rather, they are claiming that the early Christians gave Jesus these titles because of their "experience" of what he did, and that these titles originally said nothing about who or what Jesus really *was.* Thus, in the very next sentence the article states, "In other words, such designations originally expressed not so much the nature of Christ's inner being in relation to the being of God, but rather the pre-eminence of his soteriological function [i.e., his function in bringing salvation] in God's redemption of mankind."[2]

Finally, later in the booklet the same article is quoted as saying that, according to Karl Rahner, "while *theos* ["God"] is used in scriptures such as John 1:1 in reference to Christ, 'in none of these instances is "theos" used in such a manner as to identify Jesus with him who elsewhere in the New Testament figures as "ho theos," that is, the

Supreme God'" (p. 28). Then the booklet cites with approval the article's argument that one would expect the New Testament to say that Jesus was God more frequently if this was important to confess.

However, what the booklet fails to report is that the article notes[3] that Karl Rahner admitted that Jesus was called *theos* in Romans 9:5; John 1:1, 18; 20:28; 1 John 5:20; and Titus 2:13. The JWs admit that this is so in the three verses listed from the Gospel of John, but they deny that the other texts apply *theos* to Jesus. After all, these other texts would then call Jesus "the God who is over all" (Rom. 9:5), "the true God and eternal life" (1 John 5:20), and "our great God and Savior" (Titus 2:13). How Rahner could admit that Jesus was given those titles and deny that he was being called *ho theos* ("the God") is difficult to understand, to say the least.

What modern scholars think about the New Testament's teaching regarding Jesus is interesting, but hardly decisive. Both JWs and evangelical trinitarians agree that modern critical biblical scholarship, with its denial of the inspiration and reliability of the Bible and its attempts to deny the supernatural, miracle-working Jesus of the Bible, is apostate and unreliable. It is therefore unfortunate that the Witnesses quote out of context from these scholars against trinitarianism.

"The Word Was God"

In John 1:1 we read, "In the beginning was the Word, and the Word was with God, and the Word was God" (KJV, NASB, and others). The NWT translates the last clause of this verse to read "and the Word was a god." Several translations are cited in the JW booklet in support of this rendering, and a few scholars are quoted in apparent agreement with the

Witnesses' interpretation of this verse as teaching that Jesus was a second, lesser god.

In 1987 I submitted to the Watchtower Society an invitation to critique a book manuscript dealing in large part with John 1:1. I promised to include their critique in the book as an appendix. No one even responded to this offer. The same invitation was extended to other JWs who claimed to be competent in the study of Greek, and they also did not respond. The book has since been published as *Jehovah's Witnesses, Jesus Christ, and the Gospel of John.*[4] In this chapter I will simply summarize some of the main points that I made in that book—points that this new booklet published by the Watchtower Society does not mention.

The JWs reason that the Word cannot *be* "God" and also be "*with* God," since "someone who is 'with' another person cannot be the same as that other person" (p. 27). But trinitarians agree, in this sense: they hold that the statement "the Word was with God" means that the Word was with the person commonly known as "God," that is, the Father, while "the Word was God" means that the Word was himself God by nature, as much God as the Father, without being the same person as the Father.[5]

The booklet argues that because "there is no article ["the"] before the second *theos* at John 1:1... a literal translation would read, 'and god was the Word'" (p. 27). This is said to be further indicated by the fact that the word *theos* in John 1:1 is a "predicate noun" that precedes the verb and does not have the definite article. Examples are given of other verses in the Bible exhibiting this pattern and translated with the indefinite article "a" in front of the noun. These examples are said to show that "Colwell's rule"[6] cannot prove that *theos* in John 1:1 cannot be translated "a god" (pp. 27, 28).

This line of reasoning may sound valid, but it actually confuses several issues. First, even Jehovah can be called "a God" in the Bible, in passages using the exact same construction in Greek. (It should be noted that there is no difference in substance between "a god" and "a God," because modern English is one of the few languages that can even make this distinction.) For example, in Luke 20:38 in the NWT we read that Jesus said, concerning Jehovah, "He is *a God*, not of the dead, but of the living...." Here "a God" translates *theos* without the article and before the verb, just as in John 1:1. Thus, even if one wanted to translate *theos* in John 1:1 as "a god," that would not disprove that he is the true God.[7]

Second, the parallel texts cited by the JW booklet as having the same Greek construction are noteworthy in that none of them gives the Greek noun a weaker or different meaning than if it had the definite article in front of it. For example, "a spirit" (Mark 6:49) is no less a spirit than one called "the spirit"; the devil is as much a "liar" and a "manslayer" (John 8:44) as anyone could be! Moreover, not mentioned by the JWs is the fact that elsewhere in the New Testament, whenever the word *theos* is used in the same construction, it always clearly refers to the true God (Mark 12:27; Luke 20:38; John 8:54; Phil. 2:13; Heb. 11:16). Thus, the fact that the Word is called *theos* in John 1:1 in this construction does not make him *any less* God than the Father.[8]

Third, it is by no means necessary to translate nouns in such constructions with the indefinite "a" or "an," as even the Witnesses admit when they say that "when the context *requires* it, translators may insert a definite article in front of the noun in this type of sentence structure" (p. 28, emphasis added). Since the one argument from the context offered by JWs (that the Word was *with* God and therefore could not *be* God) has been shown not to *require* their interpretation, it is improper to translate it as they have done.

Fourth, the context actually supports very strongly the conclusion that the Word was God, not a secondary, inferior god. The verse begins by saying that the Word was existing "in the beginning," meaning that the Word was already in existence when time itself began. Thus, the Word was not a creature, but was in fact eternal.[9] Also, verse 3 states that everything that has ever come into existence has done so through the Word; as was pointed out in chapter 5, this must mean that the Word was the Creator and therefore God.

Fifth, by translating "a god" the JWs have made the Bible contradict itself. As was shown earlier in this book, the Bible flatly denies over and over that there are any other real, true gods besides the one true God. Since the Word is clearly not a false god, he must be a true God—that is, the *only* true God, Jehovah.

Thus, the problem is mostly not with the insertion of "a" before the word *god;* it is mostly the word *god* itself, with a lower-case "g," which in English (unlike most other languages) suggests to the reader a lesser god. Translating "a God" in English in this context would also imply this idea, but not nearly so clearly, and only because in the context "a God" would seem to be contrasted with "God." But in Greek the difference between *ton theon* ("God" in the middle part of the verse) and *theos* ("God" at the end of the verse) does not suggest this sort of shift in meaning. This can be seen by reading other passages in the New Testament where *theos* appears in the same context both with and without the definite article, yet with no change in meaning (John 3:2; 13:3; Rom. 1:21; 1 Thess. 1:9; Heb. 9:14; 1 Peter 4:10–11).[10]

A translation that perhaps brings out the difference better than any other is this: "In the beginning was the Word, and the Word was with the Deity, and the Word was Deity.'' The only problem with this translation is that we don't normally translate *theos* as "Deity"; otherwise, this is probably the most accurate translation in English.[11]

It should also be mentioned that the booklet continues the JWs' practice of quoting out of context from scholarly sources. Most notable is their use of an article in the *Journal of Biblical Literature* on John 1:1. The booklet goes so far as to claim that the *JBL* article says that the Greek construction of John 1:1 "indicates that the *logos* can be likened to a god" (p. 27). This is absolutely false. What Philip Harner—who wrote the *JBL* article—actually said was that had John written *ho logos ēn theos* (translating word for word, "THE WORD WAS GOD") this would have meant "that the *logos* was 'a god' or a divine being of some kind," but that John did *not* write this! Instead, Harner points out, John wrote *theos ēn ho logos* (translating word for word, "GOD WAS THE WORD"), which he concludes means that the *logos*, "no less than *ho theos,* had the nature of *theos.*"[12] In other words, John could have said that "the Word was a god" by changing his word order, but he did not, preferring instead to say emphatically that the Word was God as much as the person called "God" with whom he existed in the beginning.

Another scholar, John L. McKenzie, is quoted out of context as saying, "Jn 1:1 should rigorously be translated... 'the word was a divine being'" (p. 28). The JW booklet implies that calling the Word "a divine being" makes him less than Jehovah. Yet on the same page McKenzie calls *Yahweh* (Jehovah) "a divine personal being"; McKenzie also states that Jesus is called "God" in both John 20:28 and Titus 2:13 and that John 1:1–18 expresses "an identity between God and Jesus Christ."[13]

"My Lord and My God"

The Gospel of John begins (1:1) and ends (20:28, except for ch. 21, which reads as an appendix) with the confession of two of Jesus' original disciples that Jesus Christ is God. In John 1:1 the apostle John, whose faith in Jesus was perhaps the strongest of all the disciples, states that Jesus Christ was God in the very beginning of time. In John 20:28 Thomas, whose faith among the disciples (other than Judas) was probably the weakest, also confesses that Jesus Christ was his very own Lord and God.

The JWs' discussion of this verse shows that they are not sure what to make of it: "To Thomas, Jesus was like 'a god,' especially in the miraculous circumstances that prompted his exclamation. Some scholars suggest that Thomas may simply have made an emotional exclamation of astonishment, spoken to Jesus but directed to God" (p. 29).

Neither explanation is very convincing. To take the first, assuming that Jesus was not God, had Thomas called Jesus his "god" in an involuntary exclamation prompted by the "miraculous circumstances," this would have been nothing short of superstitious and would have called for a rebuke (*compare* Acts 14:11–15).

As for the second explanation, the idea that a devout Jew in the first century would cry something like "O my God!" out of astonishment is an anachronism, reading back into the Bible something that is common in our culture but virtually unknown in Thomas's culture. First-century Judaism regarded any careless or thoughtless use of the words *Lord* and *God* as bordering on blasphemy. Moreover, while in our modern culture people often do exclaim "O my God!" or "O my Lord!" when confronted with something shocking, neither in our culture nor in any other do people exclaim "My Lord and my God!" in that sort of situation.

The JWs reason that whatever John 20:28 means, it cannot mean that Jesus is Jehovah God, for three reasons: (1) John 17:3 says "that Jehovah alone is 'the only true God'"; (2) Jesus in John 20:17 referred to Jehovah as his God; and (3) John 20:31 states that the Gospel was written to show that Jesus was the Son of God, not God (p. 29). But this reasoning is self-defeating. If Jehovah is the only true God, and he is, then Jesus cannot be Thomas's God unless Jesus is also the only true God; otherwise, Thomas is worshiping a false god. The fact that in the immediate context Jesus called the Father "my God," far from showing that Jesus was a lesser god, shows that by calling Jesus "my God" in John 20:28, Thomas was giving Jesus the highest honor possible. And the fact that Jesus is the Son of God supports, not contradicts, the fact that he is also God—otherwise John 20:28 contradicts 20:31.

Two other points may be made. The language of "my Lord and my God" is found elsewhere in the Bible, with reference to Jehovah (Ps. 35:23; Rev. 4:11). Second, at least one JW publication has stated that when a Hebrew (that is, an Israelite or Jew) says "my God," he means Jehovah.[14] These facts give further confirmation that Thomas was speaking of Jesus Christ as the one true God, Jehovah.

"The Mighty God"

Isaiah 9:6 calls Jesus "Mighty God," which JWs argue implies that he is a lesser god because he is not called "Almighty." They further argue that "to call Jehovah God 'Almighty' would have little significance unless there existed others who were also called gods but who occupied a lesser or inferior position" (p. 28).

This reasoning is proven faulty by the following considerations. First, in Isaiah 10:21, just one chapter later in the same book, *Jehovah* is called "the mighty God." Thus, the context not only disproves the idea that the expression "Mighty God" means a lesser god, it supports the interpretation that it identifies Jesus as Jehovah.

Second, the expression "Almighty God" has great significance even though this Almighty God is also the only genuine, real God. For example, those who hold to *deism* claim to believe in only one God but deny that the one God is Almighty, holding instead that God is unable to change the course of history. The JWs' argument here, in fact, betrays their false view of God. They think "Almighty" means that God is simply the mightiest, the one who is mightier than all other mighty beings (including an unknown number of "mighty gods"). The biblical view is that "Almighty" means that God possesses "all might," that he is "all-mighty," the One for whom nothing is impossible (Luke 1:37). Thus, since God is the all-mighty God and the only true God, Jesus cannot be the Mighty God unless he is the true, all-mighty God himself, Jehovah.

"I Am"

In John 8:58 in the NWT the words of Jesus read, "Before Abraham came into existence, I have been." Most translations render the last part of this verse "I am" rather than "I have been." The expression "I am" has generally been understood to echo the words of Jehovah in Exodus 3:14 ("I AM WHO I AM" in most translations). The JWs argue that this cannot be because (1) Exodus 3:14 should be translated "I will be what I will be" or the like; (2) the Greek expression in John 8:58 is better translated "I have been" or the like; and (3) the Jews' surprise at Jesus' claim to have seen Abraham despite being less than fifty years old (John 8:57) is said to show that in verse 58 Jesus was simply asserting that he was older than Abraham (p. 26).

This argument rests mostly on half-truths. The second half of my book, *Jehovah's Witnesses, Jesus Christ, and the Gospel of John*, which the Watchtower Society and several individual JWs were invited to critique, is a thorough study of this verse that shows that the JW interpretation of it is faulty.[15] Here I will just make a few simple points.

First, while it is true that the expression in Exodus 3:14 is probably better translated "I will be what I will be," this is not the whole story. For one thing, this is really not that different in meaning from "I am who I am." Both imply that God is completely self-contained, that he alone determines what and who he is and what he will do, and that just being who he is will be sufficient to meet the needs of his people.[16] Also, the Septuagint, the main Greek translation of the Old Testament current in the first century, translated Exodus 3:14 "I am the One who is" *(egō eimi ho ōn)*, and readers of John's Gospel who were versed in the Septuagint might easily have noticed a parallel to Exodus 3:14 in the Greek of John 8:58, where the words "I am" are also *egō eimi*. So it is not at all unlikely that there is a connection between the two passages.[17]

Second, the translation "I am" of Jesus' words *egō eimi* in John 8:58 is definitely to be preferred over "I have been" or any such rendering. I have discussed the grammatical issues thoroughly in my previous book.[18] Here I would simply point out that the words *egō eimi* appear throughout the Gospel of John, always (when spoken by Jesus) carrying great significance, and are always (even in the NWT) translated "I am" (John 4:26; 6:35, 48, 51; 8:12, 24, 28, 58; 10:7, 11, 14; 11:25; 14:6; 15:1, 5; 18:5, 6, 8). These "I am" sayings are obviously intended to be related to one another, and this connection is lost if *egō eimi* in John 8:58 is translated "I have been." Thus the translation "I am" found in the majority of translations is correct, rather than the past-tense renderings found in other translations.

Also lost in the NWT is the connection between John 8:58 and the "I am" sayings of Jehovah in the Book of Isaiah. Most biblical scholars who have written extensively on the subject agree that these "I am" sayings in Isaiah are even more relevant to John 8:58 than the words of God in Exodus 3:14. The NWT renders these sayings as "I am the same" or "I am the same One," which further hides the parallel. In Hebrew they read literally "I [am] he," and in the Septuagint were translated *egō eimi,* "I am" (Isa. 41:4; 43:10; 46:4; 52:6; *see also* 45:18).[19]

Third, the JWs' claim that in John 8:58 Jesus was merely asserting that he was older than Abraham does not fit the context. It is true that the Jews pointed out that he was not yet fifty (v. 57). However, this was not simply a request for his true age (since no first-century human could possibly have lived in Abraham's day, roughly 2,000 years previously!). The actual topic of discussion throughout chapter 8 is the identity of Jesus (John 8:12, 19, 24, 25, 28, 53). Thus the real question was who did Jesus, a man in his prime, think he was, that he could claim to have seen Abraham?[20]

In this context Jesus does not merely claim to be older than Abraham. Gabriel or any of the angels, or even the devil, could have claimed as much. Are we really to believe that Gabriel or the devil could say, "Before Abraham came into existence, I am"? The truth is that this statement was a claim to be *eternal,* to exist without beginning, in contrast to Abraham, who had a beginning. This fits the context in which Jesus was claiming to be greater than Abraham (vv. 52–57). It also fits the precise language used, which contrasts "came into existence" with "am."[21] This same contrast, using even the same words, is found in the Septuagint translation of Psalm 90:2, which says to Jehovah: "Before the mountains were *brought into existence. . .* from age to age *you are.*"[22] As JWs recognize that in Psalm 90:2 the language used indicates that Jehovah is everlasting, so too they ought to recognize that Jesus' language in John 8:58 indicates the same thing about himself.

"Equal with God"

Philippians 2:6 in the NWT reads concerning Christ, "Who, although he was existing in God's form, gave no consideration to a seizure, namely, that he should be equal to God." The JWs argue that here Paul is saying that Jesus was not equal to God and did not even consider trying to make himself equal to God. They recognize that this verse has been understood as saying that Jesus was equal to God but did not consider equality with God something to which he needed to hold fast, but they argue that the word *harpagmos* ("a seizure," NWT) cannot have that meaning. In support they quote Ralph Martin's comment, "It is questionable, however, whether the sense of the verb [*harpazō*, the verb from which *harpagmos* is formed] can glide from its real meaning of 'to seize,' 'to snatch violently' to that of 'to hold fast'" (p. 25).

However, Ralph Martin (whose earlier book on Philippians 2:5–11 has made him widely regarded as the leading authority on the interpretation of this passage[23]) offers an interpretation of this key verse that differs from that of the JWs. First, Martin states that "*being in the form of God* looks back to our Lord's pre-temporal existence as the Second Person of the Trinity."[24]

Next, he examines the possible interpretations of the phrase "did not regard equality with God a thing to be grasped" (NASB). The traditional views were that it meant

Christ was equal with God and did not consider that wrong, or that he was equal with God but did not cling to that status. These views are found inadequate.[25] This leaves us with the view that Christ, when he was "in God's form," did not try to seize or forcibly attain equality with God.

So far this may seem to support the Witnesses' view; but in his earlier book Martin makes an important distinction that the JWs miss. Martin relates "equality with God" in Philippians 2:6 to "equal with God" in John 5:18. On the basis of parallel expressions in the Jewish rabbinical literature, he understands both expressions to mean, not the substantial equality of nature with God that Christ as the second person of the Trinity had from eternity, but an independent "equality" by which he would have been a rival or rebellious God. Martin concludes that Christ was by right *(de jure)* equal to God in the sense of possessing God's nature, and could have demanded that his creatures honor him as such; but he chose to seek equality with God in fact *(de facto)*, not by demanding it independently of his Father, but instead by humbling himself as a man and allowing the Father to exalt him.[26]

That this line of reasoning is essentially correct may be seen from the surrounding context. The JW booklet itself draws attention to one feature of this context. In Philippians 2:3–5 Paul says that we are to follow Christ's example of humility and "let each esteem others better than themselves" (v. 3 *Douay,* as quoted in the booklet, p. 25); from this statement the booklet concludes that Christ "esteemed God as better than himself" and thus denied being in any sense equal with God (pp. 25–26). But this conclusion is the exact opposite of the point being made. Paul is not telling Christians that they are *actually* inferior to one another (obviously, since not every Christian can be inferior to every other Christian!), but that they ought to treat one another *as if* the other person was more important or better. Then he gives his supreme example: Christ was actually not inferior to God and could have claimed the right to be treated as equal to God; but he chose instead to make himself God's slave and humble himself as a man to the point of death (vv. 7–8). This fits the doctrine of the Trinity exactly, since it teaches that the three persons are equal in nature but are so perfect in love that they seek to glorify each other rather than themselves.

The other main feature of the context that indicates that Jesus was truly God is the fact that in verses 9–11 Paul says that God highly exalted Jesus and gave him the "name which is above every name," that every one should confess that Jesus is *Lord.* As Ralph Martin points out, the language used here (paraphrasing the words of Jehovah in Isa. 45:23) and the use of the word *Lord* indicate that the "name which is above every name" is *Lord,* the Greek New Testament substitute for Jehovah.[27]

The JWs usually argue that this is impossible because if Jesus were Jehovah, he would have always had that name, and would not need to be "exalted" by God or "given" that name. But this argument misses the point, which is that the Son of God humbled himself by becoming a man, and he put himself thereby in the position of needing to be exalted by the Father and shown by the Father to be in truth the Lord, Jehovah. Just as Jesus was the Son of God, the Messiah, and the Lord at least from his birth (Luke 1:35; 2:11), yet was declared or shown to be all those things by his resurrection (Acts 2:36; Rom. 1:4), so also he was Jehovah, God in the flesh all along, but was publicly exalted by the Father as such after being raised from the dead (Phil. 2:6–11).

Thus Jesus Christ was neither an inferior god who was required, because of being a mere creature, to do whatever

God demanded, nor a second, independent God who asserted his rights as God over the world he created. Instead, he was the humble Son of God, possessing God's nature and having every right to recognition as such, but voluntarily choosing out of his great love to humble himself before the Father and to serve God and man as the Savior of the world, depending on the Father to exalt him according to his perfect will.

Jesus as God: Not Just a Title

Besides the passages discussed so far in this chapter, there are four other texts in the Bible not discussed in the JW booklet that clearly testify to the truth that Jesus Christ is Jehovah God. These texts also show why it is so important to acknowledge Jesus as God. These four texts are Titus 2:13, "of our great God and Savior, Christ Jesus"; 2 Peter 1:1, "our God and Savior, Jesus Christ"; 1 John 5:20, which calls Jesus Christ "the true God and eternal life"; and Hebrews 1:8–12, which calls Christ both *God* and *Lord.*

The translation of the first two of these texts is often disputed. Thus, the NWT translates them as "of the great God and of [the] Savior of us, Christ Jesus" (Titus 2:13) and "our God and [the] Savior Jesus Christ" (2 Peter 1:1). But the addition of the word *the* in brackets (indicating it is not found in the original Greek), attempting to make "God" a different person than the "Savior," is incorrect (despite the fact that some translators have done so). These passages follow exactly the same construction as is found in the expressions "our Lord and Savior Jesus Christ," "the Lord and Savior Jesus Christ," and "the Lord and Savior" (2 Peter 1:11; 2:20; 3:2, 18). This construction in Greek connects two nouns with the Greek word for *and (kai)* and places a definite article "the" in front of the first noun but not in front of the second (e.g., "the Lord and Savior"). In fact, every occurrence of this construction, when the nouns are singular and are common nouns describing persons (Father, Son, Lord, Savior, brother, etc.), uses the two nouns to refer to the same person.[28] Thus, the construction used, and especially the way Peter uses it elsewhere, strongly supports the conclusion that in 2 Peter 1:1 Jesus is called "God."

In Titus 2:13 the context supports this interpretation also. First, the Greek word for *manifestation* (or *appearing* in some translations) is always used by Paul with reference to Christ alone (2 Thess. 2:8; 1 Tim. 6:14; 2 Tim. 1:10; 4:1, 8; Titus 2:13). This makes sense, since Jesus Christ is the visible representation or manifestation of God (John 1:18; Col. 1:15; Heb. 1:2; etc.). Second, three times in Titus the expression "our Savior" is used with reference to God (1:3; 2:10; 3:4) and then immediately after with reference to Christ (1:4; 2:13; 3:6). In all six of these texts, the words "our Savior" have the Greek definite article *the* in front of them, except for Titus 2:13 (a point missed in English since the expression "our Savior" in English cannot have the word *the* in front of it). The simplest explanation, if not the only one, for this omission is that the definite article in front of "God" ("the great God and Savior of us") serves as the article for both nouns.

1 John 5:20 ends, "…his Son, Jesus Christ. This is the true God and life everlasting" (NWT). Biblical scholars disagree as to whether "the true God" here applies to Jesus Christ, or to the Father whose "Son" Jesus Christ is. The JWs, naturally, insist that the Father is being called the true God. Grammatically this is just possible (though

not the most obvious or simplest reading), but the context indicates otherwise. The statement "this is the true God *and life everlasting*" clearly is referring to one person as both "true God" and "life everlasting." But in 1 John 1:2 Jesus Christ, who "was with the Father and was manifested to us," is identified as "the everlasting life" (NWT). Thus, in this letter John begins and ends with a reference to someone called the "everlasting life"—and at the beginning of the letter it *must* be Jesus, while at the end the grammar most naturally suggests that it is also Jesus. Both grammar and context, therefore, point most strongly to the conclusion that it is Jesus Christ who is being called "the true God and life everlasting."

These three texts show that one cannot know Jesus as "Savior," as the source of "everlasting life," without also knowing him as "our great God," "the true God." It is only because Jesus Christ is God that he can save us.[29]

Finally, Hebrews 1:8–12 is one of the most powerful passages in the Bible on the subject of Jesus as God. The opening verses of Hebrews have already declared that the Son was the "heir of all things" (v. 2a; cf. Col. 1:15–17), the one through whom everything was made (v. 2b), the "exact representation" of God's very being (v. 3a), the one who "sustains all things by the word of his power" (v. 3b) and who accomplished our salvation (v. 3c), who is better than all the angels (v. 4), and is worshiped by the angels (v. 6). Thus, the Son has already been described as in essence God, identified as the Creator, Sustainer, Owner, and Savior, and ascribed worship by the inhabitants of heaven. It should come as no surprise, then, that in verse 8 God the Father says "of the Son, 'Your throne, O God, is forever and ever...'" (translating literally).

To circumvent this plain statement, the NWT renders verse 8 as "God is your throne forever and ever...." On

merely grammatical considerations, this translation is possible, and some biblical scholars have favored this rendering. According to such a reading, the point of the statement
is then that God is the source of Jesus' authority.

However, this seems to be an unusual, if not completely
odd, way of making that point. In Scripture a "throne" is
not the source of one's authority, but the position or place
from which one rules. Thus, heaven is called "the throne of
God" (Matt. 5:34). Surely God does not derive his authority
from heaven, or from anyone or anything! But, even assuming that "God is your throne" would be understood as
having that meaning, in context this makes no sense. The
writer of Hebrews is quoting Psalm 45:6 and applying it to
the Son to show that the Son is far greater than any of the
angels. However, if all this verse means is that the Son's
authority derives from God, this in no way makes him
unique or greater than the angels, since this could be said of
any of God's obedient angels.

In any case, the next quotation from the Psalms leaves no
room for doubt. Continuing to speak about the Son, the
writer of Hebrews quotes these words (Heb. 1:10–12 NWT):

> You [at] the beginning, O Lord, laid the foundations of the
> earth itself, and the heavens are [the] works of your hands.
> They themselves will perish, but you yourself are to remain
> continually; and just like an outer garment they will all grow
> old, and you will wrap them up just as a cloak, as an outer
> garment; and they will be changed, but you are the same,
> and your years will never run out.

In the context of Psalm 102:25–27 from which this is
quoted, these words are spoken of Jehovah. If the Son was
not Jehovah, then it was illegitimate for the writer of
Hebrews to quote these words about Jehovah and apply
them to Jesus to try to prove that he was greater than the

angels. Moreover, what these verses say about Jesus can only be true of Jehovah—namely, that he created the heavens and the earth (cf. Isa. 44:24) and is unchanging and eternal by nature.

Thus, the entire first chapter of Hebrews testifies that the Son, Jesus Christ, is himself God. This is not merely a matter of possessing the title *God*, though he does have that title. It is a matter of his being the One who creates, sustains, and saves us; the One to whom worship is due; the One who deserves to rule on the throne forever and ever. These things are all true only of Jehovah God, and it is zeal for the greatness and uniqueness of Jehovah God that demands that these things can be admitted to be true of Jesus only if he is in fact Jehovah.

Jesus as Jehovah

The amount of material in the Bible supporting the teaching that Jesus Christ is Jehovah God is actually quite staggering. Here we can summarize only some of the remaining highlights.

Mention has already been made of Philippians 2:9–11, which says that Jesus has been given "the name which is above every name," the name *Lord*, or Jehovah. Even clearer is Romans 10:9–13. Here we are told to confess Jesus as *Lord* (vv. 9–10), confident that no one trusting in him, that is, in Jesus, the rock over which the Jews stumbled, will be disappointed (v. 11; cf. 9:33), because he is *Lord* for both Jew and Greek, rich to all who call upon him for salvation (v. 12). Then verse 13 concludes that whoever will call upon the name of the *Lord* will be saved. In context, this must be Jesus, because he is the Lord on whom all must call to be saved, as verses 9–12 have said; but the NWT translates "Lord" here as "Jehovah," because it is a quote from Joel 2:32, where the original Hebrew has the divine name! Thus Jesus is here identified as Jehovah. Similar is 1 Peter 2:3, which is nearly an exact quotation from Psalm 34:8, where the *Lord* is Jehovah; but from verses 4–8 it is also clear that the *Lord* in verse 3 is Jesus.[30]

Besides the name *Jehovah* and the title *God,* Jesus has other titles belonging exclusively to Jehovah. Jesus is *the first and the last* (Rev. 1:17; 22:13; cf. Isa. 44:6). He is *the King of kings and Lord of lords* (1 Tim. 6:15; Rev. 17:14; 19:16). Used in a spiritual, ultimate sense, Jesus is revealed to be God by his having the titles *Savior* (Luke 2:11; John 4:42; 1 John 4:14; cf. Isa. 43:11; 45:21–22; 1 Tim. 4:10), *Shepherd* (John 10:11; Heb. 13:20; cf. Ps. 23:1; Isa. 40:11), and *Rock* (1 Cor. 10:4; cf. Isa. 44:8).

Jesus also receives the honors due to Jehovah God alone. He is to receive the same honor given to the Father (John 5:23). He is to be feared (Eph. 5:21), to receive absolute love (Matt. 10:37), and to be the object of the same faith we have in God (John 3:16; 14:1). He receives prayer (John 14:14; Acts 7:59–60 compared with Luke 23:34, 46; Rom. 10:12–13; 1 Cor. 1:2; etc.), worship (Matt. 28:17; Heb. 1:6), and sacred service (Rev. 22:3).

Jesus also possesses the unique characteristics, or attributes, of God. He is exactly like God, the very image of his Father (Col. 1:15; Heb. 1:3). All the fullness of God's nature dwells in Christ in bodily form (Col. 2:9). In another book the JWs make this interesting comment on Colossians 2:9: "Being truly 'divinity,' or of 'divine nature,' does not make Jesus as the Son of God coequal and coeternal with the Father, any more than the fact that all humans share 'humanity' or 'human nature' makes them coequal or all the same age."[31] Of course people who share human nature are not the same age, but that is in keeping with the fact that all human beings have a beginning. But the point is that just as a human son is just as "human" as his father, so Jesus Christ, who is said in Colossians 2:9 to be fully "divine," is therefore no less divine than his Father.

The Bible also names specific attributes unique to God that are possessed by Christ. He is self-existent (John 5:26); unchanging (Heb. 1:10–12; 13:8); eternal (John 1:1–2; 8:58; 17:5; Col. 1:17; Heb. 1:2, 12), omnipresent, an attribute that JWs deny even to God (Matt 18:20; 28:20; Eph. 1:23; 4:10; Col. 3:11); and beyond human comprehension (Matt. 11:25–27).

This last point bears emphasizing. The biblical teaching that Jesus Christ is Jehovah, the Lord of all, God in the flesh, is found throughout the New Testament. Yet it remains hidden from those who seek God on their own terms, who demand that he be comprehensible to them. No one can know that Jesus Christ is the Lord Jehovah apart from the revelation of the Holy Spirit (1 Cor. 12:3). Fittingly, it is to the subject of the Holy Spirit that we now turn.

8

▲▼▲▼▲▼▲▼▲▼▲▼▲▼▲▼▲▼▲▼▲▼▲▼▲▼▲▼▲▼▲

Is the Holy Spirit a Force?

The JWs believe that there is no person called "the Holy Spirit." Instead, they believe that "holy spirit" is an impersonal force. We shall consider the biblical teaching relevant to this question shortly. But first it will be helpful to relate this teaching to the Witnesses' beliefs about God.

Why the Jehovah's Witnesses' God Needs a Force

According to the Witness booklet, holy spirit "is a controlled force that Jehovah God uses to accomplish a variety of his purposes. To a certain extent, it can be likened to electricity, a force that can be adapted to perform a great variety of operations" (p. 20). God uses this "active force" to create, enlighten his servants, transmit information to his people (like radio waves), energize people to be bold and to do things normally beyond human ability, and execute his judgments (pp. 20–22).

But why does the JWs' God need such a force? For the simple reason that they believe that Jehovah is not omnipresent. They believe that God has a body, composed of spirit, and is located somewhere up in the sky, far away no doubt, but still somewhere in the physical space-time universe.[1] This is contradictory to the Bible, which teaches that God *created* the heavens (Gen. 1:1; Ps. 102:25–27; Isa. 44:24; Heb. 1:10–11; etc.); if God created the heavens, where was his "spirit body" before he created them? The Bible teaches that God cannot be contained in the heavens (1 Kings 8:27; Isa. 66:1; Acts 7:48–49), that he fills the universe (Jer. 23:23–24; Acts 17:27–28), and that likewise Christ, who is also God, is present everywhere (Matt. 18:20; 28:20) and fills all things (Eph. 1:23; 4:10; Col. 3:11). But the JWs deny these truths. In their view God is limited to whatever location his spirit body occupies.

Consequently, the God worshiped by the Witnesses needs a lot of help to get his will done. He depends greatly on his legions of angels to carry messages for him, to come down to earth and find out what is happening and then return to inform him, to execute his plans, and the like. (By contrast, orthodox Christianity teaches that God does not need his angels to do anything, but simply pleases to work through them that they might enjoy being a part of his great work in the universe.) But for whatever he does on his own, he must work through the impersonal force called "holy spirit." Unlike his own being, "God's spirit can reach everywhere" (p. 21). Thus, when Psalm 139:7–12 says that Jehovah himself is everywhere, the Witnesses understand this to mean that he is able to exert his influence everywhere through the agency of his force.

It must always be kept in mind that JWs do not believe in the same kind of God as orthodox Christians, just without the Trinity. They do not believe in the same kind of God at all. The orthodox God is absolutely infinite, the Creator of space, time, matter, and energy, transcending all finite bounds, omnipresent, omnipotent, omniscient. The Witnesses' God is *none* of these things.

A curious puzzle arises when one asks about the nature of God's "force." It is not God, according to the Witnesses, since it is an impersonal force that God *uses*. Nor is it a created thing, since God used it to create all things. Where, then, did it come from? If it is neither Creator nor created, neither God nor created thing, what is it?

It would seem that there are only two ways to answer this question (which the JWs do not seem to have addressed). This force might be considered an energy source that emanates from God's own spirit body. But this raises the troublesome question as to whether God's supply of this force is infinite. If he has a finite body composed of a limited amount of spirit, can he run out of spirit? Or does he recycle it somehow? The other way to answer the question is to say that this force coexists alongside God through all eternity, and he uses it for his own purposes. But then we have something outside God that exists forever independent of God—something that he did not create and, therefore, that he cannot destroy. Both explanations fail to help with another question—namely, how God, who is located somewhere very far away, is able to control this force from so many trillions or more miles away.

These may seem like silly questions, but they constitute real problems for JWs who insist that they be able to understand the God they worship. The point is that in their zeal to avoid mystery, they end up in what can only be called nonsense.

The trinitarian God has no such problems. The Holy Spirit is nothing less than God himself. God is present everywhere, so he has no problem controlling his works. He needs no force outside himself to do his works, nor does he need to emanate some of his own energy to places far from his presence in order to "be there."

One thing ought to be clear so far—the trinitarian God, for all his mysteriousness, is by far a greater God than the one worshiped by JWs. Such a great God commands so much more respect, honor, and praise, and he is the source of so much greater confidence in his ability to do what he promises.

But what does the Bible say about the Holy Spirit? Does it teach that the Holy Spirit is a person, or not? Is the Holy Spirit God, or something God uses?

That the Holy Spirit is a divine person can be seen from Acts 5, where Peter first tells Ananias that he has "lied to the Holy Spirit" and then that he has "lied not to men, but to God" (Acts 5:3, 4). The NWT renders "lied" as "played false," which is not quite so obviously personal, perhaps to soften the force of the words "lied to the Holy Spirit." But otherwise the implication is clear enough. The Holy Spirit can be lied to and is equated with God.

There are actually numerous references to "the Holy Spirit," or often simply "the Spirit," that clearly imply his personhood. In this chapter we will look first at those passages that the JW booklet mentions, and then turn to a few major passages it does not mention.

The Name of the Holy Spirit

Matthew 28:19 says that Christians are to be baptized "in the name of the Father and of the Son and of the Holy Spirit." Since the Father and the Son are known to be persons, and since the word *name* is used here with reference to the Holy Spirit as well, it would seem that the Holy Spirit is here being spoken of as a person.

The booklet offers two points in rebuttal to this argument. First, they state that "the word 'name' does not always mean a personal name, either in Greek or in English," and give as an example the expression "in the name of the law" (p. 22). No examples from biblical Greek, however, are given. In fact, the Greek word for "name" (onoma) is used some 228 times in the New Testament, and except for four place-names (Mark 14:32; Luke 1:26; 24:13; Acts 28:7; see also Rev. 3:12) always refers to persons. Reading the modern idiom "in the name of the law" back into Matthew 28:19 is simply anachronistic.

Second, the booklet quotes A.T. Robertson's Word Pictures in the New Testament as saying that the word name is used "for power or authority." That is true, of course, but it stands for the power or authority of someone, never some impersonal force. An impersonal force cannot have authority; only a person can. Radio waves, electricity, energies, forces, and the like, have no authority or personal power.

That the trinitarian interpretation of Matthew 28:19 fits the text better than the JW interpretation is easily seen. According to the Witnesses, Jesus here commands Christians to be baptized in the name of the eternal personal God Jehovah, the created angelic inferior god Jesus, and the impersonal active force that God somehow uses. According to trinitarians, Jesus told us to baptize in the name of the divine persons of the Father, the Son, and the Holy Spirit.

The Other Helper

In John 14–16 Jesus speaks at great length about the Holy Spirit, calling him the "Helper" or "Comforter" (Greek paraklētos). The only point made about this passage's teaching on the Holy Spirit by the JW booklet is a trivial one. It points out that the use of masculine pronouns for the Holy Spirit does not prove personality but is dictated by grammar, since paraklētos is a masculine noun. Although some Christian writers have made too much of these masculine pronouns, there is much more in the passage that testifies to the Spirit's personhood.

First of all, there is Jesus' use of the expression "another Helper" (John 14:16). The word *another* clearly implies that there is a first "Helper," Jesus Christ; and in John's first letter he explicitly calls Jesus our "helper with the Father" (1 John 2:1 NWT). Since the first Helper, Jesus Christ, is a person, one would normally expect the other Helper to be a person also. This expectation is confirmed by the use of the word *paraklētos,* which seems to have been used almost always in the sense of a legal assistant, personal representative, advocate, defender, or helper.[2] In context Jesus is saying that although he is going away, the disciples will not be left alone because the Spirit will come to be another Helper.

Shortly after making this promise, Jesus tells the disciples that "the helper, the holy spirit, which the Father will send in my name, that one will teach YOU all things and bring back to YOUR minds all the things I told YOU" (14:26 NWT). Here we are told that the Holy Spirit will be sent in Jesus' name; one does not normally speak of sending a force or energy, and certainly not of sending an impersonal force in someone's name! And then we are told immediately that the Holy Spirit will teach the disciples everything they need to know.

Later Jesus tells the disciples, "When the helper arrives that I will send YOU from the Father, the spirit of the truth, which proceeds from the Father, that one will bear witness about me; and YOU in turn, are to bear witness..." (15:26–27 NWT). Again, the Helper is sent; he "arrives," something that is also not normally said of a force (say, of a radio wave); and he performs yet another personal function, that of bearing witness to Christ. It is striking that the disciples are told to bear witness after receiving the witness borne by the Spirit; the implication, once more, is that both acts of bearing witness are personal acts.

Jesus' most extended discussion of the Helper's ministry comes in chapter 16. Here Jesus tells the disciples that when he goes away, he will "send" the Helper to them (16:7). When the Helper "arrives he will give the world convincing evidence" concerning sin, righteousness, and judgment (16:8 NWT). Further, "when that one arrives, the spirit of the truth, he will guide YOU into all the truth, for he will not speak of his own impulse, but what things he hears he will speak, and he will declare to YOU the things coming. That one will glorify me, because he will receive from what is mine and declare it to YOU" (16:13–14 NWT). Again, the Holy Spirit is sent and arrives; he comes to bring evidence to the world's attention of its sin, of God's standard of righteousness, and of their impending judgment unless they repent. He guides the disciples into all the truth. He does not speak on his own initiative, but says whatever he hears from Jesus and the Father, seeking only to bring glory to Christ. Surely saying that an impersonal force will say nothing on its own but only what it hears is absurd. The Holy Spirit is here described as humble, self-effacing, and concerned only for the glory of the Son. There is no more personal attribute than humility!

It is admittedly possible to pick out *some* features of this passage's teaching about the Holy Spirit and imagine how they might be said of an impersonal force. But all of these features will be most easily explained if the Spirit is regarded as a person, and some of the things said about the Spirit simply cannot make sense on any other interpretation.

The Holy Spirit versus Unholy Spirits

The JWs admit that the word *spirit* can refer to a person. Thus, they recognize that Jehovah is a person; they regard

Jesus as a spirit, and also as a person; they hold that the devil and his demons, all evil spirits, are also persons; and they believe that some Christians will be resurrected as spirits and live in heaven as spirit persons.

It must be admitted as possible, then, that "the Holy Spirit" is also a person. As we have seen, there is some evidence for this conclusion. Another important line of evidence comes from the fact that the Bible contrasts the Holy Spirit with unholy spirits. There are at least three passages in the New Testament where this contrast is explicit.

In Mark 3:22 the scribes accuse Jesus of casting out demons "by means of the ruler of the demons" (NWT), that is, with the help of the devil. After arguing that it is self-contradictory to say that Satan casts out Satan (vv. 23–27), Jesus warns them, "Truly I say to YOU that all things will be forgiven the sons of men, no matter what sins and blasphemies they blasphemously commit. However, whoever blasphemes against the holy spirit has no forgiveness forever, but is guilty of everlasting sin." Mark then adds, "This, because they were saying: 'He has an unclean spirit'" (vv. 28–30 NWT).

There are two things here of note. The first is that the Holy Spirit can be blasphemed. This does not by itself prove either that the Holy Spirit is a person or that he is God, since, for example, "the word of God" can be blasphemed (Titus 2:5). However, the fact that this is the worst sort of blasphemy that can be committed suggests strongly that the Holy Spirit is God himself. Also, in the parallel passage in Matthew Jesus says that "whoever speaks a word against the Son of man, it will be forgiven him; but whoever speaks against the holy spirit, it will not be forgiven him..." (Matt. 12:32 NWT). Here, speaking against the person of the Son of man is contrasted with speaking against the Holy Spirit, which is considered far worse. The implication is that the Holy Spirit is a divine person.

Second, and perhaps even more important, the *Holy Spirit* is contrasted with an *unclean spirit* (Mark 3:29–30). That is, to the charge that Jesus had an unclean spirit, Jesus responds that in fact he has a *holy* spirit—*the* Holy Spirit, in fact. As the unclean spirits that Jesus cast out were personal entities and not impersonal forces, so also the Holy Spirit by whose power Jesus cast them out was also a person.

Another passage containing a similar contrast is 1 Timothy 4:1, which reads, "But *the Spirit* explicitly says that in later times some will fall away from the faith, paying attention to *deceitful spirits* and doctrines of demons" (NASB). The contrast between "the Spirit" and "deceitful spirits" invites the conclusion that "the Spirit" is a person, not a force; and this understanding is reinforced by the fact that "the Spirit" is said to have spoken.

This text so clearly indicates the personhood of the Spirit that the NWT mistranslates it to read, "However, the *inspired utterance* says definitely that in later periods of time some will fall away from the faith, paying attention to misleading *inspired utterances....*" That this is a mistranslation can be seen from the fact that the "deceitful spirits" are linked with "doctrines *of demons,*" indicating that these "spirits" are actual evil beings and not merely utterances.

Another text where a similar mistranslation of "spirit" occurs is 1 John 4:1–6, where the phrase "inspired expression" is used eight times in place of the simple word "spirit" (*pneuma*, as in all of the above passages). What makes this significant in this context is that in the previous verse John talks about "the spirit which he gave us" (1 John 3:24 NWT), that is, the Holy Spirit. His point in 1 John 4:1, then, in warning Christians not to "believe every spirit," is that there are counterfeit spirits claiming to be from God but which are really from the devil. This implies that the Spirit whom God has given to every Christian, "the Spirit of truth" (1 John 4:6, cf. John 14:17; 15:26; 16:13), is a personal spirit, just as is the demonic "spirit of error" (1 John 4:6).

Person or Personification?

Almost all of the biblical material presented above for the personhood of the Spirit is ignored by the JW booklet (and much more that this book does not discuss). But in principle Witnesses have an explanation for it all. It is simply "personification"—the practice of describing an impersonal reality as if it were personal. The booklet points out that wisdom has children (Luke 7:35), sin and death are called "kings" (Rom. 5:14, 21), water and blood, along with the Spirit, are called "witnesses" (1 John 5:8).

It is true that abstract and impersonal realities are occasionally personified in this way. But no one ever gets confused by these figures of speech. No one thinks sin, which elsewhere is explicitly defined abstractly as acts of unbelief (Rom. 14:23) or as failure to do what is right (James 4:17) or as transgressions of the law (1 John 3:4), is a person. No one thinks that death or water or blood are persons. No one thinks that wisdom is a person, although some people think that in Proverbs "wisdom" sometimes pictures Christ figuratively. On the other hand, most people (including most antitrinitarians) who have read the New Testament have thought the Holy Spirit to be a person, and for good reason, as has been explained.

Moreover, personification as a metaphorical device can explain only so much. Except perhaps in poetical and highly symbolic forms of literature—especially Psalms and Proverbs, but also Daniel and Revelation—there do not appear to be other examples of impersonal realities personified over and over again in such a sustained fashion as the Holy Spirit is "personified" in John 14–16. Wherever impersonal realities are personified, as has been noted, the fact that they are impersonal is already well known. To say, then, that all of these biblical passages that speak of the Holy Spirit as a person are mere personifications of an impersonal force, when this is never clearly indicated in the Bible, is to imply that the Bible is misleading us concerning the nature of the Holy Spirit.

The Witnesses, however, believe that there are such indications in Scripture of the impersonal nature of the Holy Spirit. The Watchtower booklet gives some representative examples of these indications (pp. 21–22). We may comment briefly on these as examples of the mistaken reasoning by which JWs deny that the Holy Spirit is a person.

The Holy Spirit supposedly is sometimes equated with God's power (Judg. 14:6; Luke 5:17). But actually neither of these texts *says* that the Holy Spirit is God's power. In fact, Judges 14:6 does not actually use the word *power* or any synonym (the TEV reading "the power of the LORD made Samson strong" is a paraphrase), and Luke 5:17 does not mention the Holy Spirit.

The Holy Spirit appeared in the form of a dove (Mark 1:10); but this no more proves the impersonality of the Holy Spirit than the fact that Jehovah (or his angel) appeared to Moses as a fire in a bush (Exod. 3:2–4) proves that Jehovah (or his angel) is not a person.

The Holy Spirit is compared with fire (Matt. 3:11; Luke 3:16); but as we have just seen, God appeared as fire to Moses, and the Bible elsewhere says (speaking figuratively, of course) that God *is* fire (Deut. 4:24; 9:3; Heb. 12:29).

Being filled with the Spirit is compared with getting drunk on wine (Eph. 5:18); true enough, but the same

Epistle tells Christians that we are to be filled *with God* (Eph. 3:19; 4:10). The whole point of Ephesians 5:18 is that we should give control of our lives over to no impersonal substance (such as wine), but be controlled only by God in his Spirit.

The Holy Spirit is supposedly "included among a number of qualities" (p. 22) in 2 Corinthians 6:6; but by this reasoning the Holy Spirit should be a quality, not a force.

In sum, these arguments show not that the Holy Spirit is an impersonal force, but that he acts in ways that are not easily pictured as the actions of a human being. Because the Holy Spirit works in the inner beings of countless individuals, works invisibly, and generally goes unnoticed, he invites comparison to impersonal forces in figures of speech and symbolic manifestations. But that he is not himself an impersonal force has been clearly revealed through the teaching of Jesus Christ in John 14–16, Mark 3, Matthew 28:19, and elsewhere.

9

▲▼▲▼▲▼▲▼▲▼▲▼▲▼▲▼▲▼▲▼▲▼▲▼▲▼▲▼▲▼▲

Trinitarianism
in the New Testament

So far we have seen that the doctrine of the Trinity developed in the early church in response to reinterpretations of the Bible's teaching that were heretical and unbiblical—even by the JWs' thinking, for the most part. Trinitarianism stands for the absolute oneness of God and for the belief that God alone created us and alone saves us. We have seen evidence that Jesus Christ is God, and that the Holy Spirit is a person who is also God. And we have developed these biblical teachings in full harmony with the Bible's clear distinctions between the Father and the Son, as well as its distinguishing of the Holy Spirit from the Father and the Son.

What we have so far, then, are the *elements* of the doctrine of the Trinity. But does the Bible encourage us to think of God as Father, Son, and Holy Spirit? Is this threefoldness evident in the Bible itself, or has it been imposed on the Bible artificially? In this chapter we shall see that the very structure of New Testament teaching is trinitarian, despite the lack of the theological terms used in later trinitarian formulations.

Trinitarian "Prooftexts"

Attention is usually focused in this context on verses such as Matthew 28:19, where Jesus commands baptism "in the name of the Father, and of the Son, and of the Holy Spirit." Also commonly mentioned are 1 Corinthians 12:4–6 and 2 Corinthians 13:14. And these are important texts.

It is interesting to note the JW booklet's comment on these texts: "Do those verses say that God, Christ, and the holy spirit constitute a Trinitarian Godhead, that the three are equal in substance, power, and eternity? No, they do not, no more than listing three people, such as Tom, Dick, and Harry, means that they are three in one" (p. 23). They further point out that "Abraham, Isaac, and Jacob," as well as "Peter, James, and John," are mentioned together frequently, "but that does not make them one."

These illustrations, however, hardly help the Witnesses' case. For one thing, all three examples of groups of three people are just that—groups of three *persons*, each no more and no less a person than the other. In fact, the expression "Tom, Dick, and Harry" is generally used to mean "any three men," with the presumption that one is pretty much the same as another! So also Abraham, Isaac, and Jacob are three patriarchs, and Peter, James, and John are three apostles. If anything, these illustrations show that it is more likely that "Father, Son, and Holy Spirit" refers to three persons of the same basic kind—in this case, three divine persons—than that it refers to an almighty God, a created angel, and an impersonal force!

To buttress their denial that these texts speak of the Trinity, the JWs quote from M'Clintock and Strong's *Cyclopaedia*, which does deny that this group of texts can "prove, by itself, that all the three belong necessarily to the divine nature, and possess equal divine honor" (p. 23).

However, in the very next sentence the *Cyclopaedia* states that this can be proved from a "second class of texts," namely, the texts we have discussed in previous chapters that speak of Jesus and the Holy Spirit as God.[1]

The reasons given by M'Clintock and Strong for denying that Matthew 28:19 clearly speaks of three divine persons are less than persuasive:

> For *(a)* the subject into which one is baptized is not necessarily a *person,* but may be a *doctrine* or *religion. (b)* The person in whom one is baptized is not necessarily God, as 1 Cor. 1,13, 'Were ye baptized in the name of Paul?' *(c)* The connection of these three subjects does not prove their *personality* or *equality.*[2]

In response we may point out the following:

(a) While no examples are given, it may be admitted that one might speak of baptism into a doctrine or religion. However, the expression "baptizing them *in the name of*" removes all doubt that persons are meant. Besides, we know that the Father and the Son are persons, and therefore it is most natural to take the Holy Spirit as also a person—and most unnatural and strained to deny this conclusion.

(b) In 1 Corinthians 1:13 Paul is expressing horror at the thought of people baptizing others in his name. He is not saying that baptism may be done in the name of a creature such as himself—rather, he is objecting to such a practice. Moreover, we already know that the Father is God, so that the coordination of the Son and the Spirit with the Father tends to support their being God also.

(c) The mere connection of Father, Son, and Holy Spirit does not *of itself* prove that each is a divine person in one God; but the command to baptize in their name, taken together with the fact that the first two are known to be persons, *at least* proves that the Holy Spirit is a person, and strongly implies that all three are God.

Regarding 2 Corinthians 13:14, the JW booklet (p. 23) quotes the following statement from the *Cyclopaedia:* "We could not justly infer that they possessed *equal authority,* or the same nature." In isolation, this is probably true. But the *Cyclopaedia* says, in the first part of the same sentence, that "we might infer, from the parallelism of the third member of the passage with the two former, the *personality* of the Holy Spirit."[3]

One other common prooftext for the Trinity ought to be mentioned. When Jesus is baptized, the Holy Spirit symbolically descends on him as a dove, and the Father announces that Jesus is his Son (Matt. 3:16–17; *see also* Mark 1:10–11; Luke 3:21–22; John 1:32–34). The JW booklet argues that the descent of the Spirit on Jesus at his baptism implies "that Jesus was not anointed by spirit until that time" (p. 23), but this is not said. Are we to believe that John the Baptist was filled with the Spirit from his mother's womb (Luke 1:15), while the Son of God was devoid of the Spirit until he was about thirty years old? Are we to believe that a mere human, which according to the Witnesses Jesus was, lived a sinless life for about thirty years without the help of the Holy Spirit? The fact is that the Holy Spirit's descent on Jesus was not for him to become actively present in Jesus' life for the first time, but to mark *publicly* the beginning of Jesus' ministry and manifest to the world that the Spirit was indeed on Jesus.

These prooftexts, then, do support the belief that Father, Son, and Holy Spirit are three persons, and also lend some support—though probably not absolute proof—to the belief that these three persons are God. But their chief importance does not lie in their constituting isolated prooftexts for the

Trinity as a complete doctrine. No one verse tells us everything about God. The importance of these texts is in demonstrating that the New Testament writers did think along "trinitarian" lines, without the formal vocabulary, of course, of later trinitarian theology.

But it is not just in a few prooftexts that this threefoldness, this trinitarian pattern, is to be found. On the contrary, it pervades the New Testament.

A Survey of New Testament Trinitarianism

The story of the New Testament is the story of the acts of the Father, the Son, and the Holy Spirit. The central figure is, of course, the Son, Jesus Christ; but he comes to reveal the Father and to reconcile us to the Father and, after his ascension, sends the Holy Spirit to glorify the Son and lead people to know the Son as Lord, to the glory of the Father. This trinitarian structure is threaded all the way through the New Testament, from Matthew to Revelation, from Jesus' birth to the final revelations given to the last of the apostles.

The Trinity in the Gospels

We may begin by tracing this pattern in the Gospels. Jesus Christ, the Son of God the Father, is conceived by the power of the Holy Spirit (Luke 1:35). As has been noted, when Jesus is baptized, the Holy Spirit descends on him and the Father announces that Jesus is his Son (Matt. 3:16–17; Mark 1:10–11; Luke 3:21–22; John 1:32–34). Jesus faces temptation in the wilderness as the Son of God with the fullness of the Holy Spirit (Luke 4:1–12). He promises the disciples that they will not have to prepare what to say when brought on trial for their faith, because the words will be given to them by the Spirit of their Father (Matt.

10:20), by Christ (Luke 21:15), and by the Holy Spirit (Mark 13:11; Luke 12:12). Jesus comes to prepare the way for the coming of the Spirit, who will fill those who believe in Christ with life overflowing with worship for the Father (John 4:10–26; 7:37–39). After Jesus has ascended, the Father will send the Holy Spirit on behalf of the Son (John 14:16–17, 26; 15:26; 16:7). The Father, Son, and Holy Spirit will all dwell in the believer (John 14:17, 23). Everything that the Father has is the Son's, and everything the Spirit reveals to us comes from the Son (John 16:14–15). As the Father sent the Son, so the Son sends the disciples in the power of the Holy Spirit (John 20:21–22), with the commission to baptize in the name of the Father, Son, and Holy Spirit (Matt. 28:19).

The Trinity in Acts

In the Book of Acts the same pattern emerges in the life of the church. After reminding the disciples of the Father's promise to send the Holy Spirit in the Son's place (Acts 1:4–5), Jesus charges them to leave the future in the Father's hands as they bear witness to Jesus in the power of the Holy Spirit (1:7–8). Jesus then ascends, and on Pentecost he sends the promised Holy Spirit from the Father (2:33). Those who are called by God and respond in repentant faith are baptized in Jesus' name and receive the Holy Spirit (2:38–39). Ananias and Sapphira are judged for lying to the Holy Spirit, to God, and to the Spirit of the Lord (5:3, 4, 9). The apostles preach Jesus as Christ and Savior to those who receive the witness of the Holy Spirit through them (5:30–32). In his last moments Stephen, the church's first martyr, was filled with the Holy Spirit and saw Jesus at the right hand of God (7:55–56). After hearing that God anointed Jesus Christ, the Lord of all, with the Holy Spirit (10:36–38), Cornelius and his family received the Holy

Spirit, exalted God, and were baptized in Jesus' name (10:44–48; 11:15–18). Later Peter, who had preached to Cornelius, would recount that God granted salvation and the gift of the Holy Spirit to the Gentiles through the grace of the Lord Jesus (15:8–11). Paul charged the elders in Ephesus to care for God's church, which he purchased through Christ's blood and over which the Holy Spirit made them overseers (20:28). The Book of Acts closes with Paul's quoting of the words spoken by the Holy Spirit through Isaiah concerning the unbelief of the Jews, and then turning to preach God's kingdom and teach about the Lord Jesus Christ to the Gentiles (28:25–31).

The Trinity in Paul

This trinitarian pattern becomes even more evident in Paul's Epistles, though space permits mentioning only some of the highlights. We begin with the letter to the Romans. Paul preaches the gospel of God concerning his Son who was vindicated as such by his resurrection through the Spirit of holiness (Rom. 1:1–4). God's love has been shown to us in the death of his Son and placed in our hearts through the Holy Spirit (Rom. 5:5–10). God sent his Son to set us free from death and make us alive in his Spirit (Rom. 8:2–4), who is both the Spirit of God and the Spirit of Christ (Rom. 8:9–11). By his Spirit dwelling in us we are adopted sons of God in union with Christ and thus are privileged to know God as Father (Rom. 8:14–17).

Turning to Paul's letters to the Corinthians, the apostle says that Christians are washed, sanctified, and justified in the name of Jesus and in the Spirit of God (1 Cor. 6:11). Despite the diversity of gifts, there is the same Spirit, Lord, and God (1 Cor. 12:4–6). The Spirit distributes the gifts as he wills in Christ's body, so that every member is where

God desires (1 Cor. 12:11–12, 18). God establishes Christians in Christ, the Son of God, and gives us the Spirit (2 Cor. 1:19–22). The new covenant is a ministry of the Spirit, transforming us into the glorious image of the Lord in Christ (2 Cor. 3:6–8, 14–18). Paul concludes 2 Corinthians with the benediction, "The grace of the Lord Jesus Christ, and the love of God, and the fellowship of the Holy Spirit, be with you all" (2 Cor. 13:14 NASB).

Most of Paul's other letters exhibit similar patterns. God justifies us and gives us his Spirit through faith in Jesus Christ (Gal. 3:8–14). God sends the Spirit of his Son into our hearts so that we might be adopted sons of God (Gal. 4:4–7). Christians worship God in his Spirit and glory in Christ Jesus (Phil. 3:3). By God's choice, Christians have salvation in Christ and a transformed life in the Holy Spirit (1 Thess. 1:3–6; 2 Thess. 2:13–14). God saved us through the Holy Spirit whom he poured out on us through Jesus Christ (Titus 3:4–6).

Paul's letter to the Ephesians, however, may be one of the highest expressions of trinitarian faith in the New Testament. God chose and predestined us to salvation through Jesus Christ and sealed us in the Holy Spirit (Eph. 1:3–14). On this basis Paul prays that the God of Jesus Christ may give to Christians the Spirit of wisdom and revelation (1:15–17). Of Christ he writes, "for through Him we both have our access in one Spirit to the Father" (2:18 NASB) and are becoming "...a holy temple in the Lord ...a dwelling of God in the Spirit" (2:21–22 NASB). Paul again prays, this time asking the Father to strengthen us through his Spirit so that Christ may dwell in our hearts and we thereby know Christ's love fully (3:14–19). He reminds us that there is "one Spirit... one Lord... one God and Father of all" (4:4–6). We should therefore not grieve the Holy Spirit, but forgive others as God has forgiven us in Christ (4:29–32). We are to be filled with the Spirit, giving thanks to God the Father in the name of our Lord Jesus Christ (5:18–20).

The Trinity in the Rest of the New Testament

The rest of the New Testament also testifies to a fundamental trinitarian faith (though not a formalized doctrine of the Trinity). The word of salvation was spoken through the Lord, and God bears witness to it now through gifts of the Holy Spirit (Heb. 2:3–4). Christ offered himself as a blood sacrifice for our sins through the eternal Spirit to God (Heb. 9:14). Those who reject Christ in effect kill the Son of God all over again, insult the Holy Spirit, and therefore face certain judgment by God (Heb. 10:28–31; also 6:4–6). Peter states that we are foreknown by God the Father, sanctified by the Spirit, and sprinkled with Christ's blood (1 Peter 1:2). John states that Christians have confidence before God as they believe in Christ and remain in union with Christ through God's Spirit (1 John 3:21–24; 4:13–14). Jude encourages Christians to pray in the Holy Spirit, keep themselves in God's love, and hope in the mercy of Jesus Christ (Jude 20–21). In Revelation the Son of God claims authority from his Father and calls on his hearers to heed "what the Spirit says to the churches" (Rev. 2:18, 27–29).

Christian Faith Is Trinitarian Faith

The purpose of this survey is not to claim that each one of these passages, taken in isolation, "proves" the Trinity. Rather, the point is that taken together, along with the evidence considered in previous chapters for the deity of Christ and the Holy Spirit, they constitute a solid cumulative case for the position that the faith of the New Testament is trinitarian. By that is meant, not that it is necessary to know or accept the word *Trinity* to be a Christian, but that the Christian faith revealed in the New Testament *is* what the doctrine of the Trinity says it is. To be a Christian, it is not necessary to know or understand the formal expressions of trinitarianism that were the result of centuries of reflection on the New Testament in the light of heretical distortions of that faith. However, to be a Christian, one must not reject the faith that the doctrine of the Trinity was constructed to safeguard.

Moreover, to be a responsible Christian—not merely in the sense of obtaining personal salvation, but in the sense of being a full partner with the rest of Christ's church in the fellowship and service of Christ—one must accept the doctrine of the Trinity. Not to accept the Trinity, after the church carefully and cautiously developed it in response to attacks on its faith, is to deny that Christ preserved his church through the ravages of heresy and apostasy, and thereby implicitly to insult Christ (Matt. 16:18; Jude 3–4).

10

▲▼▲▼▲▼▲▼▲▼▲▼▲▼▲▼▲▼▲▼▲▼▲▼▲▼▲▼▲

Worship God as He Has Revealed Himself

The JWs are correct when they say that we ought to "worship God on his own terms" (*Should You Believe in the Trinity?*, p. 30). But by rejecting the doctrine of the Trinity, the Witnesses are actually rejecting God's revelation of how he wishes to be worshiped.

Everlasting life, as the Witnesses correctly point out, depends on knowing God (John 17:3). But the Bible makes it clear that no one can know God apart from knowing Christ as he really is. Indeed, Jesus in John 17:3 indicates that salvation is dependent on knowing him as well. The apostle Paul, who as a Pharisee seemingly had every reason to be confident that he knew God and had his approval (Phil. 3:4–6), considered "all things to be loss on account of the excelling value of the knowledge of Christ Jesus my Lord" (3:8 NWT). This is strange if Jesus was simply the greatest of creatures, but fitting if, as we have seen, Jesus was God. That Paul viewed Jesus as God is indicated in this very passage by his statement that as Christians we "have our boasting in Christ Jesus" (v. 3 NWT), even though Paul himself insisted on the Old Testament principle, "But he that boasts, let him boast in Jehovah" (2 Cor. 10:17 NWT).

Thus, knowing Christ *is* knowing God. "If YOU men had known me, YOU would have known my Father also; from this moment on YOU know him and have seen him" (John 14:7 NWT). Not only that, but no one can know the Father apart from Christ: "I am the way and the truth and the life. No one comes to the Father except through me" (v. 6 NWT). "Everyone that denies the Son does not have the Father either. He that confesses the Son has the Father also" (1 John 2:23 NWT). If the Son is a creature, it ought to be possible to know God apart from that creature. But no one can, because Jesus is God.

Moreover, no one can honor God who does not honor Christ. In fact, all men are to "honor the Son just as they honor the Father" (John 5:23a NWT). The Bible contains many warnings against creature worship; it also contains many commands to exalt, honor, worship, love, praise, fear, and serve Christ, and warnings against those who deny that Christ is "our only Owner and Lord" (Jude 4 NWT). (How can Jesus be our *only* Owner and Lord if he is not God?) But the Bible never warns against exalting Jesus too highly. No one is ever censured for giving him an honor he does not deserve. That is because Jesus Christ has "the name above every name" (Phil. 2:9), is "far above every government and authority and power and lordship and every name named, not only in this system of things, but also in that to come" (Eph. 1:21 NWT). It is therefore impossible to exalt Jesus too highly.

Confusing the Issue

The JW booklet *Should You Believe in the Trinity?* charges that the doctrine of the Trinity "has confused and diluted people's understanding of God's true position" (p. 30). However, the doctrine of the Trinity is not the source of the confusion about the nature of God. Rather, it was the denial of the simple biblical teachings about the Father, Son, and Holy Spirit that led to a bewildering variety of theories about Christ and the Holy Spirit and thereby called for a careful, precise formulation of the meaning of the Bible's teaching about God.

It is interesting that the JW booklet cites Catholic theologian Hans Küng as asking, "Why should anyone want to add anything to the notion of God's oneness and uniqueness that can only dilute or nullify that oneness and uniqueness?" (p. 30). In context Küng is expressing sympathetically the attitude toward the doctrine of the Trinity expressed *by Muslims,* followers of the religion of Muhammad.[1] Küng goes on to note that Muslims are just as scandalized by the New Testament teaching that Jesus is the Son of God.[2]

In fact, it is the JW teaching that there are many gods, Jehovah being the greatest and Jesus the second greatest, that dilutes or nullifies the oneness and uniqueness of God. To hold that Jesus Christ is the one who directly made all things, who sustains all things, who did the great work of dying for our sins, who has "all authority in heaven and on earth" (Matt. 28:18), and who will judge the world—and then to deny that Jesus is actually God, certainly detracts from God's uniqueness and glory. Only trinitarianism, which affirms all the glorious things said about Jesus in the New Testament, but also affirms that Jesus is the Son of God, sent by the Father, and made known to us by the Holy Spirit, preserves the oneness and uniqueness of God in the light of the New Testament.

Thus, the JWs like most antitrinitarians, agree with Jews and Muslims, and disagree with Christians, as to the meaning of saying that God is one. In rejecting the Trinity, they are rejecting what makes the Christian conception of

God unique compared to all non-Christian and sub-Christian conceptions.

The Witnesses also claim that belief in the Trinity has led to various evils—specifically, unbiblical exaltation of Mary, persecution of antitrinitarians, and wars in which trinitarians kill one another. This claim, however, simply confuses the issue. None of these practices are in any way the result of belief in the Trinity.

The title "mother of God" used of Mary originally had nothing to do with exalting Mary. The actual word used was *theotokos*, a Greek word meaning "God-bearer." It meant that the person conceived and nurtured in Mary's womb was actually God. As we have seen, that is a biblical teaching. The expression "mother of God" often seems to imply that Mary has a position of authority over God, and of course that is false; but very few, if any, Catholics even understand it that way, and in any case the use of the expression to exalt Mary has nothing to do with the Trinity. Nor does the belief that Mary is a "mediatrix," a belief rejected by all Protestant trinitarians. The exaltation of Mary in Roman Catholicism to this near-divine position arose long after the doctrine of the Trinity and has nothing to do with it.

Also confusing the issue is the reference to trinitarians' persecution of antitrinitarians. While this *has* occurred, it was not a result of believing the Trinity, but of holding to the belief that the civil government has a responsibility to punish or even execute heretics. When and where antitrinitarians have been in power and held to a similar belief about the role of government, they have often persecuted trinitarians. Thus, the historical persecution of antitrinitarians by trinitarians, while lamentable, does not in any way disprove the Trinity.

It must be borne in mind that simply believing in the Trinity does not make a person Christian. To be a Christian, one must put one's faith in the God who is triune, not simply acknowledge him to be triune. Nor does believing in the Trinity guarantee that even a Christian's beliefs and practices will be right in all other areas.

Even less relevant is the unfortunate history of wars in which trinitarians have killed trinitarians. Whether or not we grant the premise that all participation in war is sin (a premise with which some, though not all, Christians agree), the fact that trinitarians have killed one another in war, while lamentable, is no disproof of the Trinity. At most it is proof that belief in the doctrine of the Trinity does not alone guarantee that a person's conduct, or the conduct of whole nations who subscribe to the doctrine, will be consistently Christian. But there simply is no logical connection between belief in the Trinity and participation in war. These are separate issues, and to make the truth of the Trinity somehow suspect on the basis of beliefs about participation in war is simply to confuse the issue.

Trust in the Triune God

Jehovah calls upon the world to acknowledge that "there is no other God, nor anyone like me" (Isa. 46:9 NWT). This is not simply a matter of knowing the fact that Jehovah alone is God, but of trusting in Jehovah alone as God and Savior: "Is it not I, Jehovah, besides whom there is no God; a righteous God and a Savior, there being none excepting me? Turn to me and be saved, all you [at the] ends of the earth; for I am God, and there is no one else" (Isa. 45:21b–22 NWT).

It is the trinitarian who acknowledges Jehovah as the only God and Savior by his confession that Jesus Christ is truly Jehovah, not a creature. Jesus Christ is our God and Savior (Titus 2:13; 2 Peter 1:1), and he can only be so if he is

Jehovah. But simply acknowledging this truth is not enough. We must trust in Jesus Christ as God and Savior, put our hope in him, and live in a way that honors him (Titus 2:13–14).

The good news to which the devil blinds the minds of the unbelieving is the good news about Christ, "who is the image of God" (2 Cor. 4:4). The message that we are to preach is "Christ Jesus as Lord" (v. 5). When we accept Christ as Lord, God shines in our hearts the light of the knowledge of God in the face of Jesus Christ (v. 6). It is the glorious truth about Jesus Christ that the devil hates and seeks to hide from mankind by every lie imaginable (John 8:43–44).

The doctrine of the Trinity was formulated by followers of Jesus Christ to safeguard the good news that in Jesus Christ we encounter God face to face. It was not devised to make God less understandable, or to make God so mysterious that the common people would have to depend on clergy and theologians to understand it for them, as the JWs charge. Instead, the doctrine of the Trinity was developed out of respect for God's revelation of himself. The Witnesses' doctrines about God, Christ, and "holy spirit," on the other hand, were developed not in order to represent the Bible's teaching more faithfully, but to make God understandable and comprehensible.

The choice is therefore between believing in the true God as he has revealed himself, mystery and all, or believing in a God that is relatively simple to understand but bears little resemblance to the true God. Trinitarians are willing to live with a God they cannot fully comprehend. As C.S. Lewis put it:

> If Christianity was something we were making up, of course we could make it easier. But it isn't. We can't compete, in simplicity, with people who are *inventing* religions. How

could we? We're dealing with Fact. *Of course* anyone can be simple if he has no facts to bother about![3]

To believe any doctrine — even the Trinity — is not enough. One must put his trust in the true God to whom the doctrine points. One must also turn away from those doctrines that deny "our only Owner and Lord, Jesus Christ" (Jude 4 NWT). The JWs need to seek the light of God's truth concerning Jesus Christ (2 Cor. 4:6), truth that can set them free (John 8:32) from the demands of an organization that presumes to tell them what to believe. Only Jesus Christ, not any religious organization, has the words of eternal life (John 6:68). May God the Father deliver many JWs, and people of other religions as well, "from the authority of the darkness," and transfer them "into the kingdom of the Son of his love" (Col. 1:13 NWT).

Notes

Chapter 1 Understanding the Trinity

1. *Should You Believe in the Trinity?* (Brooklyn: Watchtower Bible and Tract Society, 1989). Throughout this book, pages cited in the text refer to this booklet.

2. Frederick C. Grant, "Trinity, The," in *The Encyclopedia Americana*, Vol. 27 (Danbury, Conn.: Americana Corp., 1980), 116.

Chapter 2 The Bible and the Trinity

1. Edmund J. Fortman, *The Triune God: A Historical Study of the Doctrine of the Trinity* (Philadelphia: Westminster Press, 1972), 9.

2. Ibid., xv–xvi.

3. "Trinity," *The New Encyclopaedia Britannica: Micropaedia*, Vol. X (Chicago: Encyclopaedia Britannica, 1981), 126.

4. Johannes Schneider, in "God, Gods, Emmanuel," by Johannes Schneider, et. al., in *The New International Dictionary of New Testament Theology*, ed. Colin Brown, Vol. 2 (Grand Rapids: Zondervan Publishing House, 1976), 84.

5. E. Washburn Hopkins, *The Origin and Evolution of Religion* (New Haven, Conn.: Yale University Press, 1923), 336.

6. W. Fulton, "Trinity," in *Encyclopaedia of Religion and Ethics,* ed. James Hastings, Vol. 12 (New York: Charles Scribner's Sons, 1958), 461.

7. Ibid.

8. Ibid., 458–59.

Chapter 3 The Church and the Trinity

1. Justin Martyr, *First Apology* 63, in *The Ante-Nicene Fathers: Translations of the Writings of the Fathers down to A.D. 325*, ed. Alexander Roberts and James Donaldson, rev. ed. A. Cleveland Coxe (Grand Rapids: William B. Eerdmans Publishing Co., 1969 reprint [orig. 1885]), 1:184; hereafter cited as *ANF*.

2. Justin Martyr, *Dialogue with Trypho* 36, in *ANF*, 1:212.

3. Ibid., 128, in *ANF*, 1:264.

4. Justin Martyr, *First Apology* 6, in *ANF*, 1:164.

5. Ibid., 16, 17, in *ANF*, 1:168.

6. Irenaeus, *Against Heresies* 1.10.1, in *ANF*, 1:330.

7. Ibid., in *ANF*, 1:417.

8. Clement of Alexandria, *Exhortation to the Heathen* 10, in *ANF*, 2:202.

9. Clement, *The Instructor* 1.8, 1.11, in *ANF*, 2:227, 234.

10. Clement, *Exhortation to the Heathen* 12, in *ANF*, 2:206.

11. Clement, *Miscellanies [Stromata]* 5.1, in *ANF*, 2:444.

12. Tertullian, *De Pudicitia* 21, cited in Fortman, *The Triune God: A Historical Study of the Doctrine of the Trinity* (Philadelphia: Westminster Press, 1972), 112.

13. "Elucidations," in *ANF*, 3:629.

14. Tertullian, *Against Hermogenes* 3, in *ANF*, 3:478.

15. "Elucidations," in *ANF*, 3:629–30.

16. Tertullian, *Against Praxeas* 5, in *ANF*, 3:600–601.

17. Ibid., 7, in *ANF*, 3:601, 602.

18. Michael O'Carroll, *Trinitas: A Theological Encyclopedia of the Holy Trinity* (Wilmington, Del.: Michael Glazier, 1987), 208.

19. Hippolytus, *Against Noetus* 10, in *ANF*, 5:227.

20. Ibid., 8, in *ANF*, 5:226.

21. Ibid., 6, in *ANF*, 5:225.

22. Hippolytus, *The Refutation of All Heresies* 10.30, in *ANF*, 5:153.

23. Edmund J. Fortman, *The Triune God: A Historical Study of the Doctrine of the Trinity* (Philadelphia: Westminster Press, 1972), 58.

24. Ibid., 56.

25. Gerald Bray, *Creeds, Councils and Christ* (Downers Grove, Ill.: InterVarsity Press, 1984), 83.

26. For text and discussion, *see* ibid., 104–9.

27. Harold O. J. Brown, *Heresies: The Image of Christ in the Mirror of Heresy and Orthodoxy from the Apostles to the Present* (Grand Rapids: Baker Book House, 1988 [orig. 1984]), 116–17.

28. *The New Encyclopaedia Britannica: Macropaedia*, Vol. 16 (Chicago: Encyclopaedia Britannica, 1981), 730.

29. Brown, *Heresies*, 117.

30. Bray, *Creeds, Councils and Christ*, 109.

31. Brown, *Heresies*, 115; Rousas John Rushdoony, *The Foundations of Social Order: Studies in the Creeds and Councils of the Early Church* (Fairfax, Va.: Thoburn Press, 1978), 14–15.

32. W. Fulton, "Trinity," in *Encyclopaedia of Religion and Ethics*, ed. James Hastings, Vol. 12 (New York: Charles Scribner's Sons, 1958), 458.

Chapter 5 Is Jesus a Creature?

1. Derek Kidner, *The Proverbs: An Introduction and Commentary*, Tyndale Old Testament Commentary (Downers Grove, Ill.: InterVarsity Press, 1974 [orig. 1964]), 79.

2. *Reasoning from the Scriptures* (Brooklyn: Watchtower Bible and Tract Society, 1985), 408.

3. *See further* Larry R. Helyer, "Arius Revisited: The Firstborn over All Creation," *Journal of the Evangelical Theological Society* 31, 1 (March 1988):59–67.

Chapter 6 Does the Bible Deny That Jesus Is God?

1. *See* Norman L. Geisler and William D. Watkins, "The Incarnation and Logic: Their Compatibility Defended," *Trinity Journal* ns 6 (1985): 185–97.

2. *See* especially Robert M. Bowman, Jr., and Brian A. Onken, "Was Jesus Raised as a Spirit Creature? Dialoguing with Jehovah's Witnesses on 1 Corinthians 15:44–50," *Christian Research Journal* 10, 1(Summer 1987):7.

Chapter 7 Jesus Christ Is God

1. G.H. Boobyer, "Jesus as 'Theos' in the New Testament," *Bulletin of the John Rylands Library* 50, 2 (Spring 1968):251.

2. Ibid., 250.

3. Ibid., 253.

4. Robert M. Bowman, Jr., *Jehovah's Witnesses, Jesus Christ, and the Gospel of John* (Grand Rapids: Baker Book House, 1989), hereafter cited as Bowman, *Gospel of John*.

5. Ibid., 25–26.

6. *See* ibid., 65–69, for a discussion of Colwell's rule.

7. Ibid., 48–49.

8. Ibid., 43–53.

9. Ibid., 20–24.

10. Ibid., 60–61.

11. Ibid., 27, 63.

12. Philip B. Harner, "Qualitative Anarthrous Predicate Nouns: Mark 15:39 and John 1:1," *Journal of Biblical Literature* 92, 1 (March 1973):85, 87; *see* Bowman, *Gospel of John*, 70–73.

13. John L. McKenzie, *Dictionary of the Bible* (New York: Macmillan Publishing Co., 1965), 317; *see* Bowman, *Gospel of John*, 80–81.

14. Ibid., 133–34; citing *Aid to Bible Understanding* (Brooklyn: Watchtower Bible and Tract Society, 1971), 885.

15. Ibid., 87–132.

16. Ibid., 125–27; *see also* Robert M. Bowman, Jr., *Jehovah's Witnesses and Biblical Interpretation* (forthcoming), chapter 8.

17. Bowman, *Gospel of John*, 124–25.

18. Ibid., 87–112.

19. Ibid., 120–21.

20. Ibid., 122–24.

21. Ibid., 112–16.

22. Ibid., 117–20.

23. Ralph P. Martin, *Carmen Christi: Philippians ii.5–11 in Recent Interpretation and in the Setting of Early Christian Worship* (Cambridge: Cambridge University Press, 1967).

24. Ralph P. Martin, *The Epistle of Paul to the Philippians: An Introduction and Commentary*, Tyndale New Testament Commentaries (Grand Rapids: William B. Eerdmans Publishing Co., 1959), 96.

25. Ibid., 96–97.

26. Martin, *Carmen Christi*, 148–49; *see also* Martin, *Philippians*, 97–98.

27. Martin, *Philippians*, 105; *Carmen Christi*, 235–39, 255–57, 278–83.

28. This point is documented in Robert M. Bowman, Jr., *Our Great God and Savior* (unpublished paper, 1987), 2–8; it is available from CRI, Box 500, San Juan Capistrano, CA 92693-0500.

29. For a more detailed study of Titus 2:13, 2 Peter 1:1, and 1 John 5:20, *see* ibid.

30. *See further* Robert M. Bowman, Jr., *Jehovah's Witnesses and Biblical Interpretation* (forthcoming), chapter 8; Robert H. Countess, *The Jehovah's Witnesses' New Testament: A Critical Analysis of the New World Translation of the Christian Greek Scriptures* (Phillipsburg, N.J.: Presbyterian & Reformed Publishing Co., 1982), 34–39; D.R. DeLacey, "'One Lord' in Pauline Christology," in *Christ the Lord: Studies in Christology Presented to Donald Guthrie*, ed. Harold H. Rowdon (Leicester, England: Inter-Varsity Press, 1982), 191–203.

31. *Reasoning from the Scriptures* (Brooklyn: Watchtower Bible and Tract Society, 1985), 420.

Chapter 8 Is the Holy Spirit a Force?

1. On this and related points, see Duane Magnani, *The Heavenly Weatherman* (Clayton, Calif.: Witness Inc., 1987).

2. Georg Braumann, "Advocate, Paraclete, Helper," in *The New International Dictionary of New Testament Theology*, ed. Colin Brown, Vol. 1 (Grand Rapids: Zondervan Publishing House, 1975), 88–91; Johannes

Behm, *"paraklētos,"* in *Theological Dictionary of the New Testament*, ed. Gerhard Friedrich, trans. and ed. Geoffrey W. Bromiley, Vol. 5 (Grand Rapids: William B. Eerdmans Publishing Co., 1967), 800–814.

Chapter 9 The Trinity in the New Testament

1. John M'Clintock and James Strong, *Cyclopaedia of Biblical, Theological, and Ecclesiastical Literature* (New York: Harper & Brothers, 1881), 10:552.
2. Ibid.
3. Ibid.

Chapter 10 Worship God as He Has Revealed Himself

1. Hans Küng, *Christianity and the World Religions: Paths of Dialogue with Islam, Hinduism, and Buddhism*, with Josef van Ess, Heinrich von Stietencron, and Heinz Bechert (Garden City, N.Y.: Doubleday & Co., 1986), 112–13.
2. Ibid., 116–18. It should be noted that Küng takes a modernist critical view of the Bible, for example, denying that Jesus called himself the Son of God (p. 117).
3. C.S. Lewis, *Beyond Personality: The Christian Idea of God* (London: Geoffrey Bles, 1944), 19.

Recommended Reading

Literature relating to the Trinity is enormous. Only a few select items are mentioned here.

Beisner, E. Calvin. *God in Three Persons* (Wheaton, Ill.: Tyndale House Publishers, 1984).

Bray, Gerald. *Creeds, Councils and Christ* (Downers Grove, Ill.: InterVarsity Press, 1984).

Bowman, Robert M., Jr. *Jehovah's Witnesses, Jesus Christ, and the Gospel of John* (Grand Rapids: Baker Book House, 1989).

_____. *Jehovah's Witnesses and Biblical Interpretation* (forthcoming).

Brown, Harold O. J. *Heresies: The Image of Christ in the Mirror of Heresy and Orthodoxy from the Apostles to the Present* (Grand Rapids: Baker Book House, 1988 [orig. 1984].

Geisler, Norman L., and William D. Watkins. "The Incarnation and Logic: Their Compatibility Defended," *Trinity Journal* ns 6 (1985):185–97.

Gruenler, Royce Gordon. *The Trinity in the Gospel of John: A Thematic Commentary on the Fourth Gospel* (Grand Rapids: Baker Book House, 1986).

Juedes, John P. "Trinitarianism—a Pagan Creation? An Examination of Dr. Victor Paul Wierwille's Claim," *Journal of Pastoral Practice* 5, 2 (1981):67–82.

McGrath, Alister E. *Understanding Jesus: Who Jesus Christ Is and Why He Matters* (Grand Rapids: Academie Books—Zondervan Publishing House, 1987).

_____. *Understanding the Trinity* (Grand Rapids: Academie Books—Zondervan Publishing House, 1988).

Macleod, Donald. *Shared Life: The Trinity and the Fellowship of God's People* (London: Scripture Union, 1987).

Olyott, Stuart. *The Three Are One: What the Bible Teaches About the Trinity* (Welwyn, England: Evangelical Press, 1979).

Packer, J. I. *Knowing God* (Downers Grove, Ill.: Inter-Varsity Press, 1973).

Prestige, G. L. *God in Patristic Thought*, 2d ed. (London: S.P.C.K., 1952).

Rowdon, Harold H. (ed.). *Christ the Lord: Studies in Christology Presented to Donald Guthrie* (Leicester, England: Inter-Varsity Press, 1982).

Rushdoony, Rousas John. *The Foundations of Social Order: Studies in the Creeds and Councils of the Early Church* (Fairfax, Va.: Thoburn Press, 1978).

Warfield, Benjamin Breckinridge. *Biblical and Theological Studies*, ed. Samuel G. Craig (Philadelphia: Presbyterian & Reformed Publishing Co., 1952), especially chapters 2–5.

Wells, David F. *The Person of Christ: A Biblical and Historical Analysis of the Incarnation*, Foundations for Faith (Westchester, Ill.: Crossway Books, 1984).

Subject Index

Adam, 58
Almighty, meaning of, 97–98
angel, Jesus as, 28–29, 54
angels, as gods, 51–54
Ante-Nicene Fathers, 27–35
apostasy, 45–47
Arianism, 36–38, 40–42, 44, 59
Arius of Alexandria, 36–37, 43
Athanasian Creed, 11–15, 17, 19, 42
Athanasius, 40–43

Barth, Karl, 24
Bible, as God's Word, 19, 21
blasphemy, Jesus accused of, 86–87
Bracken, Joseph, 18
Bulletin of the John Rylands Library, 89–91

Calvin, John, 87–88
Christian Science, 46

Clement of Alexandria, 28, 30, 34–35
Constantine, 37–40
Council, of Nicea, 37–40; of Constantinople, 40, 42
Creed of Nicea, 38
creeds, purpose of, 18, 44–45

egō eimi ("I am"), 99–100
elohim, 49, 52, 55
Encyclopedia Britannica, 24, 38–39
Encyclopedia Americana, 17
Encyclopedia of Religion and Ethics, 25–26, 42–43
Enlightenment, 46
Eusebius, of Caesarea, 40; of Nicomedia, 40

Father, is Jesus' God, 15, 71–72
Fortman, Edmund, 22–24, 33

Gnosticism, 29, 35–36, 44–45, 75

149

Scripture Index

Genesis

1:1—44, 52, 112
1:8, 16—52
1:26–28—52, 80
6:1–4—56

Exodus

3:2–4—121
3:14—98–100
8:10—54
9:14—54
15:11—54

Numbers

23:19—55, 75

Deuteronomy

4:24—121
4:35, 39—50
9:3—121
32:21—51
32:39—50

Judges

14:6—121

1 Samuel

12:21—51

2 Samuel

7:14—61
7:22—54
22:32—50

1 Kings

8:23—54
8:27—112

1 Chronicles

17:20—54

2 Chronicles

15:3—51

Job

1:6—56

2:1—56

Psalms

2:7—23
8:3–8—52
8:5—51–54
23:1—109
34:8—109
35:23—97
45:6—23, 107
82—55–58
82:1—55
82:2–5—56
82:6—56
82:7–8—56–57
86:8—54
90:2—61, 75, 101
96:5—51
97:7—53
102:25–27—75, 107, 112
139:7–12—112

153